94-00701

fishboy

By Mark Richard

THE ICE AT THE BOTTOM OF THE WORLD

FISHBOY

Nan A. Talese
DOUBLEDAY
New York
London
Toronto
Sydney
Auckland

fishboy

A GHOST'S STORY

Mark Richard

Published by Nan A. Talese
an imprint of Doubleday
a division of Bantam Doubleday Dell Publishing Group, Inc.
1540 Broadway, New York, New York 10036

DOUBLEDAY is a trademark of Doubleday,
a division of Bantam Doubleday Dell Publishing Group, Inc.

Portions of this novel originally appeared, in slightly
different form, in The Ice at the Bottom of the World,
published by Alfred A. Knopf, Inc., and The Quarterly.

BOOK DESIGN BY CLAIRE VACCARO

Library of Congress Cataloging-in-Publication Data

Richard, Mark, 1955–
        Fishboy / Mark Richard. — 1st ed.
            p.   cm.
        I. Title.
    PS3568.I313F57   1993
    813'.54 — dc20   92-37196
                            CIP

ISBN 0-385-42560-0

To Pearson

God gives us time to work, angels give us money and quiet places. For their generous support I thank the Whiting Foundation, the National Endowment for the Arts, the Ernest Hemingway Foundation, PEN, and the New York Foundation for the Arts.

For quiet places, I thank Bill Smart and the Virginia Center for the Creative Arts, the New York Public Library, Anstice Carroll and 220, and especially, with love and affection, Noonie and Louis Marx.

And—to cite the names of those who have my gratitude in respect of this book—Amy, Will, Jen, Punk, Herb, Georges, Denise, and Gordon, who gave me the idea, and Nan, who saw it through. Bless you all.

M.R.

fishboy

I began as a boy, as a human-being boy, a boy who fled to sea, a boy with a whistling lisp and the silken-tipped fingers of another class. A boy with put-away memories of bedclothes bound tight about the head, knocked by a hammering fist; the smell of cigar and shoe leather and the weighted burlap bag, thrown from a car into a side-road swamp. A child born again there, slithering out of the sack, a new beginning into life, holding back water to breathe through sour mudded filth and green surface slime. Put-away memories of my gums pushed back and bloody gnawing slugroot; the ripped frog muscle spasms tickling my tongue as I ate the things almost whole, and then the all-night chorus of croaking reproach; the bitter-centered snake eggs I washed down with the stagnant sulphured water, a mushroom cap for a cup, all of it heaved back up, a slack-jawed torrent of spew splashing around my ankles, heaving up my own new creations of life in the mire, bits and pieces wiggling and squirming, convulsing, web-footed and scaled, tiny dead reptilian eyes like pretty black beads in pearl.

I remember sleeping for warmth in winter with wild dogs, the precious suckled bitch's milk in exchange for one of my ears ripped with hair for the puppies to chew. I remember sleeping with snakes for summer cool, the puncture bites of small poisons that cleared my infected eyes and sharpened my hearing so that I could hear the sneezes of rats to catch as toys for this boy I began as, with still, through it all, the prissy wrist, the toe-pinched walk, a boy, who, had he any sisters, Big Miss Magine said, should have worn their handed-down dresses. This was me as that boy, a boy who fled to sea and turned to fish, this was me waiting the length of his short life in his cartonated box, waiting for the one big boat to come in to the place where hardly any boats came.

Some boat.

Any boat.

I waited for a boat big enough to brave itself through where the sea dunes and the sand waves folded over, no channel in and no channel out, a boy at the ready with his butter-turned knife to sign aboard to slice meats like fists from shells like plates.

That boy.

I had always been that boy in the cartonated box, waiting for the purple bus to pass through places I could not pronounce with my whistling lisp, places I can whisper to you now with the ease of escaping steam, dark continent-calling places, places misplaced, place names like none in this language we share. I waited for the purple bus to travel through these places edging the round cratered lake where something large from the sky struck long ago, places where the blacktop road sinks through soft-bottomed bogs and erupts flat and dry farther on, a serpentine plumbing of the earth's thin surface, the purple bus leaning on the quicksand curves, slipped tires spinning, the exhaust pipes gurgling, the white-eyed driver mostly blind and dreaming them along the road he drove, steering the bus to where I always slept in wait.

And I always slept in my cartonated box listening in the early morning chill for the tottering of the bus into the rutted fishhouse lot, the sprung springs and ratching bad brakes, the dark faces and elbows of its passengers pressed against the windows as the women reached beneath their seats for old jars of cold fish stew cooked in stone-scoured pots, grease-streaked bags of fried pork or some night animal snared on a porch or caught in a closet. And I would always wait in my cartonated box with my thumbs tucked under my chin for Big Miss Magine and her ugly sister to unburden the bus's breaking back, wait for Big Miss Magine to wade through the air to my box, wait for her to slip her lips like a big brown frog through the hole in my box through which I watched the moon at night. And I would watch, no matter the season's turn, how the blowing slow of her big breath would blue into a settling spread of fog, her words, before she pressed her eye like a painted egg against the moon-cut hole looking in to me, her words, saying *You is mine, Fishboy, you is all mine.*

And then I could be the Fishboy, fetching in with the ones who had come on the purple bus from around the cratered lake, the lake an hour across and a minute deep, I could fetch in with these tar-colored people with the crude tattoos, the coiled mazes cut into the skin of their cheeks and foreheads with owl quills and bird beaks, these people with nothing in their houses but clothing, wooden stools, stone pots, and ghosts like me. The boy like me then would fetch in with them to haul over the piers the forty-weight baskets of fish and the bottom-dwelling shells shaped like plates and platters, dumping them all along the troughs that spilled onto the tables where the big black women sliced out fillets with thin-bladed knives, knives with just enough curve to work the flesh out of the fish with a plunge of steel and a flick of the wrist.

The shucking of the bottom-dwelling seashells was left to a red-rimmed drunkard, a soft-skulled child, and me, the human-being boy, Fishboy, Fishboy shucking the shellcut between his duties of filling baskets of fish, running in his tied-around-the-neck plastic-fronted apron, skidding barefoot across the gut-spilt floor. I watched the little flat-bottomed skiffs and shallow-draft schooners unload and pack out their cargoes with a wire basket strung from a boom, and I watched, wondering, would a big boat ever come, would a big boat ever come with room enough for me, and when one would come, it was always some frightened trawler storm-blown with a broken rudder or a bad compass, or some wrong-size schooner with old fish and illegal nets, a dangerous crew and a captain with a gun. And even then it would be me begging pardon, pleading for a chance to come aboard, to wade down into the waist-deep icy black bilge water in the hold, to dive into the filth to unstopper the draincocks and scrape away the rotten fishheads so the storage bins could dry. It would be me washing out the dark 'tween decks with a rag on a stick, stacking in the boards for more of the fifteen tons of sparkling sharp ice I would shovel, bloody-knuckling the crystals pink, praying to any god *Please let the captain see it's me, please see, it's me, the Fishboy! See! Look! Clean here, clean there, clean and right, fore and aft! See how I'll work? Let them see how I'll work until I choke on the frozen smoke . . .* and then, but always then, I would hear the black women holler from inside the long dark sheds *More fish! More fish! FishBOY!* Then up the hold ladder while the hatches clattered down, I would try to tell them how much shellcut Fishboy could shuck, one hundred and seventy-seven bushels in six hours! my lisping tongue slicing the *s*'s, and then not the captain, not the mate, not a winchman, nor even a boiler devil but the lowliest seaman whose work I had saved him from doing and done as my own would come out of some soot-nested bunk or from around the corner of some hose shack, eye-glazed and trouser-stained, saying *Get along there sissy britches, this is a union-scripted barge. I bet you got to squat to pee, little sweetness, get off now before I split you myself!* and I would be lifted up from the deck by the side of his hard-swung boot and I would sail through the air over the rail hearing his rotten rodent-tooth laugh, *Thanks for the help in the hold!* and I would slap the cold wet concrete apron of the pack-out pier next to the brimming baskets of fish and shellcut, double-stacked for me to catch up, for me to carry straining and slipping across the cutting room floor, watching out the open side of the shed the union-scripted ship casting off, throwing off its lines, and I would turn not to look, hoping anyone seeing the wet on my face would think it was only the scales thrown there by the fishes' flipping tails as I emp tied the baskets into the troughs along the cutting tables deeper into the shed darkness until the last fish would slide beneath the upheld fillet knife of Big Miss Magine, pointing at me, saying in the low black breath whisper, almost in fog, *You is mine, Fishboy, you is all mine.*

*S*oda time!
Fish*BOY!*
Lunch bags and glass jars come out with the big black women drying in the cold sun on the broken-down dock, perched on pilings like feathering blackbirds, spitting gristle, speaking that around-the-cratered-lake gobbletalk, paying me a nickel to dive down into the fillet-gutted wastewater that sluices through the cutting shed floor emptying out into the creek, paying me a nickel to dive down to where the soda machine lies at the bottom, fallen through its place on the dock and still plugged in underwater. *Get me a cold soda, Fishboy, a red one!* and

holding my breath for as long as it took I could, I could even hold it long enough to steal a cold soda for myself and sit on the bottom of the gut-watered creek, watching tiny fish feed in the clouds of waste that bloomed overhead in the water while I drank.

These were the long days in the short length of my life as the Fishboy, the sun slipping into the cratered lake like a figure eight of flame. I would make the last go-around call for fish to fillet and shells to cut, letting the big black women have their pick of the rotting fish left from the bottom of the union scripts, the shallow-draft schooners, and the local boats, letting the women take the souring fish with the milky eyes and ruined blood home, wrapped in their front-tied aprons, the women drunk on finishing the last work of the day and laughing at my whistling lisp slicing through the singsong *Finish fish! Finish fish! Take home your finish fish!* And I would shuffle dead tired, my pinched toes furrowing the sand, shuffle with my own finish fish, usually just the head and spine of some ruined carcass I would simmer into stew over a driftwood fire, back to my cartonated box, my finish fish wrapped in my apron, and I would not look back to where the purple bus's back was bending beneath the flat, worn-footed weight of its passengers climbing aboard. I would crawl inside my box and wait,

wait for the blind driver to fall asleep to drive them home, wait until I was sure the bus was gone before I would peek out of my moon-cut hole, but the bus rolled slowly over the sand and never as far as I thought, and no matter how long I waited, waited until I thought it was safe to press my eyeball to the moon-cut hole, I would always see her seeing back, in the corner of the bus's back window, the bus finally leaving the lot, always a red-blue-purple painted egg of an unblinking eyeball staring straight back into my own.

A calendar tide flooded my creek the night the tattooed man swam ashore. I had been hunkered down by my driftwood fire, sipping my finish fish stew, listening to the water surge in small places. Across the creek the rising water shifted a run-aground wreck and bats by the thousands spun up through the smokestacks like the black fur of exhaust blown from boilers stoked by ghosts. The smudge of bats was split here and there by gulls and terns making whitecaps of flight to drier roosts, and from beyond the long dunes blew in a wet mist that my firelight lit like tiers of talcum sunsets.

The flood tide brought a little breeze with it ashore and somewhere I heard a wave begin to pound a loose plank in the pack-out pier. It pounded first like a fist and then like a hoof, like a horse kicking in its stall. Water darkened the sand, pooling in puddles, sprouting from the ground in odd artesian knots.

I kicked up a sand dike around my fire and tried to finish my stew, finish fish and squash and okra from my garden, the planting seeds picked from the animal droppings edging my cartonated encampment. I had seasoned the stew with the pieces of pork gristle Big Miss Magine and her ugly sister had spit from their sandwiches into the weeds around their lunchtime pilings. It was my first crop of squash and the salt air made the fruit small and bitter.

In the dark I could hear birds filling the tops of the trees around me, wings and leaves creaking the limbs of the cypress at the water, the pines along the road, and the hardwoods in the swamp beyond. I could hear a few larger forms turning overhead. I could hear them as I ate and I did not look up. I knew what they wanted. I had felt their ivory vise of talon in my shoulder once when I was weak from a fever, swooped upon and fought over until suddenly I was weightless aloft and my eyes were full of horizon, then dropped in a dry creekbed to break my head open like a clam on stone. Heavier and stronger later, I still left something out for them, the boiled-out finish fish skin stuck on top of the crossed sticks in my garden, where also hung my plastic-fronted apron to dry. It turned in the breezes, an effigy of myself, an offering, a scarecrow to no thing, the gills in the fishhead sometimes whistling in the evening winds, and something always answered it, something always answered from deep in the swamp behind my cartonated encampment, a low-octave note that made me stoke my fire and brace my box, to keep my fingers curled around my butter-turned knife as I slept in wait of the morning's purple bus.

I sipped my stew from the old Hessian bowl I had found in a gulley and listened to the earth shoulder its water away from the moon, listened to the creek swell and the waves pound, and out there in the creek's middle something like a big fish broke and I heard a man cough and gasp, and I set down my bowl with my eyes level to the noise and picked up my knife. In the dimness I could see a man waist-high in water that I knew should have been over his head. I could see him coughing, flinging a ragged mop of seaweed hair back and forth in arcing arms of spray. He was trying to cough up something stuck lung-deep. He coughed and coughed, blowing foams of snot from his nose until he hawked up something slippery in his mouth and he spit it out, it looking like a small flounder that clapped into the creek swimming seaward.

The man began to wade to my shore, rubbing his eyes and bouncing his head from side to side releasing torrents of water from his ears. I back-crawled along the side of my cartonated box and scrambled for the foliage of my garden.

Hiding in my beanstalk leaves I watched the large man mend my fire with some cypress knees and sheets of fishwrap paper. He squatted down and I saw his arms stenciled with black tattoos and what hung between his legs was like a stillborn calf I once found washed up in the creek. The tattoos on his wrists and chins were cut with scars of what looked like shark strikes, and when he turned a leg to pick at it in the firelight there was a fresh curving sweep of leaking blood and broken-off triangles of cartilage teeth.

He coughed again and spit sizzle into my fire. He drank my water, gulped at my stew until halfway through gulping he spit the stew out and flung my Hessian bowl way up in the woods. When he stood, picking bone and scale off his tongue, his belly was scraped and muddy as if he had been dragged across the ocean floor. He reached close to me in the garden and uprooted my scarecrow sticks. Across the sticks he stretched my plastic apron and tied the corners into a crude kite. Up-ending my cartonated box, he shook out my other pos-sessions: my only other shirt, my sow's ear purse of soda nickels, and my pallet bed of pine straw stuffed into a burlap bag. He ripped my shirt and the burlap bag into strips that he tied as a tail to the kite which he bridled with the miles of gourd vines that latticed my garden.

The man shook the kite's tail into the fire to light it, and then with the seaward wind to his back, he let his toy go. I watched my shirt and bed wink away burning in bits of glow and ash. Higher and higher the man pumped the kite, feeding it lengths and lengths of vine, unraveling my garden, ripping and snatching up roots that showered me with dirt, tearing away the leaf cover where I had been hidden.

The wind took the kite and roared it from over the fishhouse to over the shipwrecks on the quay, then to beyond, and I watched my shirt and bed finish burning farther and farther like a dim star that burst into a nova when the fire blazed up the plastic front of the apron kite. It was a greasy gleaming before the scarecrow sticks caught fire high overhead, a burning cross that fell and spiked itself out on the fishhouse rooftop.

Just as the line went lax in the man's hand my snakebite-sharpened ears picked up a sound from out beyond where the sea dunes and sand waves fold over.

13

From where there is no channel in and no channel out, I heard what I saw the smiling man heard, two long pulls on a mournful ship's horn.

The tattooed man broke apart my cartonated box to feed the fire, first throwing in my walls and my front door flap. In the new glow he saw me standing in the pulled-up place where my garden had been. I could see him see me, I could see him see me as some lost child with a torn-off ear like a mongrel dog, a dirty shirt, a tiny dull blade of a knife clenched in my fist. *I can shuck seventy-seven bushels of shellcut, sir,* I wanted to say, but my tongue sliced my s's and it came out sounding like I was stammering in fear and cold.

I could see him see me as not worth the atom of energy it would take him to pinch my head off like a shrimp.

Go home, son, he said, brightening his fire with my moon-cut hole.

I looked at this man from some ship riding the calendar flood, his tar-stained feet, his shark-struck legs, his fingernails sharpened into blades, the charts of the world stenciled in his skin.

I looked and saw the deficit of my garden, the deficit of my shirt, the deficit of my cartonated box.

No sir, I thought at him. *No sir, I am on you like a tick.*

*L*ate that night, to escape the rising water, I shimmied up a fishhouse drainpipe and crawled into a vacant osprey nest. It was a saucer-shaped work of knitted twigs and sticks twisted atop the drainspout. Bird lice bit my flesh and it was a rank place of chalky dung and hatchlings' crust. It was a good roost from which to watch the sleeping tattooed man and to wait for any ship that would come up our tidal creek. I waited and watched and waited and watched until my eyes went tired and I fell asleep.

A ringing noise woke me and I wasn't sure where I was until I saw the sky red and runny in the east. There was another RING! and an answering RING! like the metal-forging noise of hammered anvil in a blacksmith's shop. It went RING! RING! and then JING! and then there was a thud of something hard, heavy, and hand-held striking something soft and firm, wood or bone. I shifted on my belly, my eyes like bird eggs on the edge of the nest.

Sometime in the night some thing had tied up to the dock below me, coal-fired, low in the water, its over-thick mooring lines gripping the pilings like fingers, the lines gripping against the suck of the outgoing calendar tide and creaking and pulling against the dock like the thing was about to heave itself out of the water and stalk the fishhouse lot. I could hear the ringing more clearly now, and for a moment two figures passed beneath a shaded red-amber lantern that lit a catwalk and stained the air with the smell of kerosene. Another lantern with a broken shade lit a trio of barrel-sized exhaust pipes, their spark-streaked smoke leaking ink to blot out the remaining morning stars. A single running light burned brown on the mast; the reflection of this thing shimmered in the creek like a coal-fired jack-o'-lantern smile.

Two figures stalked the small ship in the oily sheen of first light, two figures ringing and smashing and hammering in the ship's stern, trying to kill something with axes. At first I thought a rabid animal, or a big rat, or one of those log-sized sea snakes, something that was cowering or scrambling or twisting away from the blows of the men's steel axes, some of their blows bouncing back to their sweat-soaked and salt-worn shirt breasts, these men having such a hard time putting to rest quickly the thing they so much wanted to kill. As the slow opening sun's eye stared light into the scupper corners and waste bins, I looked for the thing from my perch in the osprey nest, thinking the thing the men wanted to kill had slipped unseen into the creek, where I wouldn't go swimming for a couple of days, or maybe had wound itself up through the rigging to the crow's nest on the mast. I could not think where the thing had gone, could not think how the thing could have escaped the ringing of the blows to smash its back or cleave its head. I was not thinking any thoughts of someone who had ever seen men fight with axes before.

The sun came close to watch. In its gray yolk of light I could see the men more clearly, beards, weary faces, clothes of rotted knots, heaving the big, block-headed axes, axes so heavy that one brawny blow could slice through a shark so cleanly and quickly that its head would snap at you as you stepped past to dress out its carcass for steaks. Axes: one easy stroke to split a man from crown to groin.

An aft cabin door blew out char-fringed faces, more miserable men in less than knotted rags, men spitting and blowing their faces into their hands, beginning to seine their lousy hair with steel brushes, crushing, the bugs they combed between black cracked nails; filthy men drawing buckets of gasoline to bathe in, taunting each other with lit matches, men moving between the swings of the block-headed axes to do their business and to watch, to climb the winches and the aft rigging, making noises like they had lost at sea their tongues to talk, low grunts of the blood-seeking sort. *Lay one in him, Lonny,* they would say, *Split him once down the middle, lay his busted guts out!* they said. *Do it, Lonny,* they said. *Do it!* they demanded.

And Lonny swung harder, his own weight thrown by the throw of his block-headed axe, a hard heave of the blade that just missed the other man and pulled Lonny forward from off his heels.

That's it, Lonny! said the men in the rigging, black spiders in the tarred woven threads, *That's it!* they said. *We'll have no more of it now!* And Lonny swung again, and missed again, his blade sunk half a head into a hatch cover. *Look it, Lonny!* they said, and the other man brought a terrific blow to the deck by Lonny's foot. *Oh, Lonny!* they said.

By the time the sun sought overhead to spread more light to see by, the two men still stalked each other on the littered afterdeck. The deck and hatches suffered scores of deep grooves and splintered gashes, the thrown blows, the near misses. Staggering, Lonny and the other man were dragging their axes now, not favoring the single-handed stroke of before but bringing the axes to bear with both fists, the blows fewer but firmer, the men's wrists strained and swollen from the glancing throws of the now dulled blades, dulled from striking steel plate and stanchion instead of flesh, dulled to bludgeon instead of to sever, dulled to bounce instead of to bite, as danger-ous now to the wielder as to the mark of the man. Lonny bled from a rout earlier, when the other man, the ship's cook, had managed him in through the aft cabin door. *Don't, Lonny!* the men had warned, *He's in home!* but Lonny had followed the fight into the cramped galley and had lost a slice of cheek through a thrown meat cleaver before hacking his way back out the bolted port hatch. *See, Lonny?* the men said.

The sun seemed wanting to stay but started slipping out beyond to extinguish itself in the round cratered lake, the sun giving its last stare so hard on the scene below, staring so hotly that it seemed to hiss as it struck the surface of the distant lake, and in that last glare of brilliance came the moment that comes in all fights men have, when they finally call up the thing that everyone has been waiting so long for, and Lonny seemed to sense that the last bright blast of sun was his for himself to see by, and taking a deep breath while the cook rolled over on his haunch from a badly thrown blow to the rail, Lonny reached back with his ax, his nose wedged in the crook of his arm which his eyes clearly glared over, he reached back like he would indeed have to pull down over his shoulder the curtain of the world around him, and yet he would do it, and he did do it, the quickest blow of the day while the cook rose to meet it and was back down again under the weight of the ax while the blade of the thing bit on.

Lonny let go of the handle. It shuddered from somewhere deep inside the cook. The men swung down from the rigging, a joke about no more greasy eggs was answered with a cuff on the ear, the men a single file of filth trudging back inside the small ship's aft cabin door. I was perched on the nest's edge out of reach of the calendar tide which had flooded the roads and kept the purple bus away that day. I was just perched, a small cannonball of boy, my chin in my knees, my ankles squeezed, watching the fighting and keeping an eye on the man asleep in my garden, the sun closing behind us a sad eye of sleep.

Lonny cradled the cook in the stern quarter where he had fallen, the cook's neck gone to rubber, his face bent up to Lonny's own. *I'm cold, Lonny,* the cook said, his arms aquiver. Lonny pulled off his shirt, looking around for more cover amidst the splintered deck and the smashed hatches.

The tattooed man stirred in the falling dark and sudden quiet, and I started slipping down the drainpipe. I meant to be on him, to be in his fading shadow when he stood.

You, said Lonny, pointing a bloody finger at me. *Get me a wrap or towel, a blanket if you have one.* Inside the fishhouse were some oyster sacks, and I meant to pitch one on deck as I passed but Lonny said to fetch it to him.

I'm so cold, Lonny, the cook said. Lonny told the

cook that it would be all right, the cook's violent shuddering arms throwing off the comforting cover of Lonny's shirt so that Lonny had to hold it down.

Bring that wrap up to me, Lonny said, and I walked a spring line aboard and swung the rail. The oyster sack seemed small when I pressed it on the cook, fitting it like a bib napkin, as if the cook, who smelled of wet herbs and old seasonings, was preparing to eat.

The cook said he was sorry to Lonny, sorry to cook his eggs so greasy, sorry to salt the coffee, sorry to make stew from boiling his apron, sorry to blow snot into the beans, sorry that he was the cook at all, saying he had always wanted to be a blacksmith but that he was frightened of horses, and Lonny said that it was all right.

The cook shuddered and I pressed the oyster sack against him to keep his inside things from sliding out.

The cook felt my pressure and looked down at me.

Never learn to cook, the cook said to me and I shook my head that I never would.

The cook said that he was cold straight down the middle, could Lonny get him a nice piece of felt blanket, and Lonny said *Sure* and held the cook tighter. Lonny did not fight the quaking arms as they rose and fell against us, Lonny letting one arm finally reach around his neck as I felt the other pull me deeper into the divide of the big split body.

I am so sorry, said the cook, and Lonny said it was all right, it was all all right, and Lonny closed us tighter inside the cook's succoring, still embrace.

*B*y the light of the lantern I held, the tattooed giant whom the men called John said *God, take from us the soul of this, your nearly split-in-two servant here, the Cook, and let him taste the Gruel and Slop of Everlasting Afterlife, that is, if he has indeed risen to serve in Your Galley, instead of broiling in Your Eternal Oven where his shipmate Lonny here who suffered his cooking thinks he deserves to go.*

Amen, said Lonny.

And God, John said, John dressed in a nightshirt of white gauze, *we are actually thankful for delivering us from his fare that gave us the shits, this cook's heart so small he cheated us at our rations, harboring that broken bag of lemon sours and that flask of lime juice when the scurvy was upon us, our gums bleeding and us swallowing our teeth; but most importantly we thank You for taking him so quickly so that he didn't suffer that much, really. How mercifully You took him from this wretched earth, no longer must he toil for his wages of sin, no*

longer is he tempted by the siren call of that blind tooth-
less woman by the side of the road to the capital. No
longer is his flesh vulnerable to skin ravages and internal
sores, shingles, bloody warts, no longer has he the fear of
contracting that parasitic worm that begins to grow out
of the end of your penis so that you have to carefully
wind it around a matchstick, careful it doesn't break
apart and die and kill you . . .

I think he had that, Lonny said.

John told Lonny to have some respect for the dead
or over Lonny's grave he would pray the label from a
venereal liniment bottle.

So God, said John, *I guess the cook is no longer*
liable in the death of that woman and that woman's prize
pig on that island we anchored off of last trip, him going
ashore to scrounge victuals, us too weak from scurvy and
hunger to lift an oar into an oarlock, and then on the
evening breeze we smelled roasted pork, and he returned
greasy-fingered and fat with a woman's rhinestone hair-
clip on his belt, us having to painfully haul in the anchor
when the natives came out in their painted war canoes.
We even tolerated him when he told us they had chased
him away from the fire before he could grab the pig but
later we saw the pork worms in his stool, the bastard, oh,
the lucky, lucky bastard, You see, Lord, there is no
meanness in how I just settle the folds in the funeral

shroud with my foot here, and here, and here and STEP AWAY LONNY! I didn't mean to set a bad example! THAT'S ENOUGH KICKING! LEAVE OFF from kicking the carcass! I said. So God, take this very, very lucky bastard from us and back into Your employ to serve up boot biscuits and snot-rag stew to Your Legion of Angels who always fail us, those bright-eyed nancies with mighty swords and lacy pants.

And one last thing, said John quietly. *Help me keep my foot on the necks of these your serpents, servants.*

And let me finally net my loved one.

And send us soon another cook, real soon, added Lonny.

Amen, said John, and we buried the cook in the mud of the creek at the mark of its lowest tide.

*B*ird lice were biting my flesh again in the morning when the big purple bus tottered into the fishhouse lot. I had heard its distant backfire, had heard its ratching bad brakes as I slumped in the osprey nest again whittling twigs with my butter-turned knife. I thinned the walls of the nest whittling, thinking it had been me who'd trussed the dead cook in a rotten canvas shroud, me who'd held the lantern in the prayer, and me who'd filled in the grave. It had been me who'd found some coarse thread to sew up Lonny's cleavered cheek, who'd brought Lonny a bucket of gasoline to bathe in, scrubbing his back with a wire brush, scrubbing so that where the skin began to show it was bright pink and raw, the dirt and grime so old and thick that it fell away like pieces of rotten hide.

And it had been me fetching John a bucket of fresh water for his face, stealing him a plug of Indian tobacco from the red-rimmed drunkard's secret fishhouse rafter stash for his pipe. It had been me sitting up with John all night watching him watch the desertions from his ship, bent men stumbling without their sea legs ashore, the weight of their sea chests crumbling them into the sand, fading across the fishhouse lot with an over-the-shoulder curse at their former captain.

And it had been me swabbing the cook's human spillage off the deck with a rag on a stick, kneeling with a brush where the stain of his insides was stubborn, my clothes smelling like a spice rack in a slaughterhouse.

For all I had done, it was me who John sent away from him when he set out on the road to gather another crew. I was following him in his shadow when he turned and said for me not to walk behind him. I walked ahead of John, and not knowing where he would turn off the road I kept looking back and he said the sight of me put him off, first thing in the morning. So then I tried walking alongside him, trying to match him stride for stride, his long lengths scissoring quickly, my pinched-toe trot so awkward once I fell against the white gauze of his nightshirt.

Go away from me and stay off my ship, he said, shaking me off like I was a humping dog. *I told you once before to go home,* he said, *now go home!* and he kicked me so I rolled in the dust of the road. Where I sat watching him walk away was an ant hole. I stuck my finger in the ant hole and said to myself that I wasn't going to take my finger out until he came back, but after a while the ants organized and were fierce, so I stood up, brushed off, and walked back to the fishhouse.

In the osprey nest I whittled and watched Lonny and what was left of some of the crew, a man who played cat's cradle with string and a man who only seemed able to cry and to say *Fuck.* I watched them dynamite the brass propeller off the old steamer bankrupt on a shoal across the quay. What other brass and fittings they could take from the wreck they took, finally shooting out the portholes with cap-and-ball pistols and a musket from the crow's nest of their ship. The noise they made sent up swarm after swarm of birds from the side road and the swamp, filling the sky with circling and bird talk, and when the men brought shotguns to the rail they felled hundreds of birds in a rain of feathers and blown-apart pieces until I heard them decide there really was not much sport to it.

The day-late tide-delayed purple bus pulled, brakes squealing, into the fishhouse lot. I cut a plug of osprey wall to watch and kept my head truantly low. They in the bus saw the small dark ship listing against the pack-out pier, the wheelhouse windows black glass and sealed. They saw the men on the ship's deck with guns, and they saw the fresh grave the tide was folding over, and I knew at least one set of eyes on the bus saw the ruined garden, the burned encampment, with no sign of Fishboy about.

Two diesel dugouts with baskets of fish and a shallow-draft oyster schooner were tied up at the dock, two dim men fetching up the schooner's cargo like sacks of rocks. There were hours of work in the cutting shed but inside the purple bus the people from around the cratered lake made fists around the fetishes that hung from their necks on string. They fogged the bus windows with their breath and drew designs against the things they saw. From their throats came high trillings and triple-time gobbles, and they shook their fists at the men on the ship and touched each other's mouths for reassurance against the memories that swept through the bus, memories longer than their lives, memories of ships with bellyfuls of tar-colored people, people linked ankle to ankle in perfect patterns like the endless imprints of the bus tires in sand, memories of how the paths around the cratered lake were first cleared by the sweep of shackle and chain across the brush, memories of fleets of ships like this one, empty holes afloat the ocean, come ashore for people's souls.

Lonny and the man who played cat's cradle with string and the crying man who said *Fuck* answered the high shouts of calling and trilling responses coming from the bus with their own ooga-boogas, cocking their gripped groins and fanning their fingers from their ears. They were doing it up until Big Miss Magine unburdened herself first from the bus, Big Miss Magine in a blue floral dropsheet dress, as one pink-bottomed big black foot planted down from the doorway step raised dust, the other foot held the tipping balance of the bad suspension, the purple vehicle rocking back and forth as she departed. Big Miss Magine waded across the fish-house lot to my burned-out encampment, her rolling turbulent wake silencing Lonny and his crewmates as it lapped them in her passing.

Hands on hips, Big Miss Magine surveyed my torn-up garden and my scorched-earth cartonated encampment. Her ugly sister came down off the bus, then the soft-skulled child, the red-rimmed drunkard, and the rest of the crater-lake crowd, gobbletalk and hissing. They took a wide path past the trawler and slid open the cutting shed doors. Roped baskets on booms swung out to the waiting dugouts and the shallow-draft schooner, the water sluice spewed into the creek clear then foul with the inner strings and organs of fish and shell. Big Miss Magine sat for a time, not as long as she could have, sifting and stirring through my ashes.

Fishboy! Fishboy! was the call below me in my bird's nest hideout. In my truant deafness I picked at the white cruds of osprey with the point of my butter-turned knife.

*L*unchtime!

Soda time!

No call for Fishboy.

There was no call for Fishboy because the soft-skulled child, the child I had built a step for so he could stand at the cutting trough and shuck for food, the soft-skulled child was stripped down and diving into the wastewater creek to fetch the cold sodas for the big black women perched on their pilings, eating from their jars and greasy bags, spitting gobbletalk gristle. The women shook their fetishes against the crew they watched roasting their fresh meat on a broken-cart fire, me chewing the inside of my cheeks against the way the smoking meat made the air smell.

I was hungry and thirsty in my hideout, and it was good-smelling meat, whatever kind of meat it was.

It was meat John had brought to them. John had come back that morning mostly asleep on the driver's bench of a wagon, the reins to the mule wrapped around his fillet-knife fingers, his nodding head snoring his chin into his chest as if to chew at the heart within.

In the mule-drawn cart were four men, two shackled together in prison blues, an idiot, and the corpse of the sheriff. There was no color in the faces of the prison-blue men. The Idiot wore a cap that he turned around and around on his head. The sheriff's corpse sat beside John on the driver's bench, its throat slit open like gills.

I was seeing how to make myself useful to John. I was seeing where I could help him bury that corpse like I had helped him bury the cook's, even already thinking of a secret hole to do it in.

I was seeing where I could help him, tell him how the red-rimmed drunkard was giving out lead sticks like the women used to stun fish, I would tell John how there was rising action going on just under where my hideout was, the red-rimmed drunkard handing out lead sticks and clubs against the crew, and how he was letting the big black women sharpen their gutting knives down to the handle on his own whetstone. I was even seeing how I, if I could just slip past Big Miss Magine, how I could come down and help unhitch the mule, like it looked like he was trying to do the wrong way, the way he was cradling the mule's head with an arm under its reins. Even I could unhitch a mule the right way, brush it down and graze it in the sea-oat patch.

I was just getting ready to slip down from my osprey nest to unhitch the mule when I did not. And it was a sound that made me not come down, a sound that made my shoulders ride up on my neck. It was the sound that John made happen when after he had whispered in the mule's quilled ear and bit it gently like an animal-mounting bite, a bite that made one of the mule's rear legs quiver and stamp slightly, the sound John made was the stem-popping sound coming from the mule's neck of John turning the mule's head impossibly to look backward to the pale-faced men and the Idiot in the cart behind him.

I swung my leg back into the nest to see what next.

The mule buckled dead-kneed in its traces as Lonny came off the ship with an ax. The pale-faced men in prison blues shackled at the wrists looked from John and the mule to Lonny coming at them with the ax, and they leapt out of the buckboard and fled to the creek.

Hey! shouted Lonny after the prison-shackled men, *can any of you cook?* but the shackled men did a three-armed creek swim and scrambled up the far shorebank.

John held the mule up by its throat and opened its chest with his fillet-nailed hand, entrail and offal spilling onto the sand, dressing the animal out. Lonny started chopping up the wagon for firewood and kindling even as the Idiot sat in it, inching away from the hacking blade.

Come on out, said Lonny as he swung.

It's an idiot, said John, stripping off the mule hide into a wet cloak.

Can it cook? said Lonny.

It's an idiot, said John, stripping the leather reins from the harness, fashioning a crude belt for his crude cloak.

What does it take to cook? said Lonny, grabbing at the Idiot to get him out of the cart.

You have always seemed real particular, said John. *How do you like my new coat?*

Get this idiot out of the cart, said Lonny.

John ripped the sheriff's bright star off the sheriff's patched pocket and pinned it to the peak of the Idiot's cap. Hoisting the sheriff's corpse on his shoulder, he clapped his leg and whistled; the Idiot came loping behind like a puppy.

The man who played with string they called Ira Dench, and Ira Dench brought down to where Lonny cooked the butchered mule a wicker basket trimmed in red-and-white checkerboard. They put seared slabs of bloody meat on china plates and passed them to the crew that John had gathered from their ship, the man who said *Fuck* and the chief engineer and his two boiler monkeys. Just the appearance of the chief engineer and his two boiler monkeys did much to frighten the red-rimmed drunkard's band of cratered lake women with their concealed lead sticks and clubs, their knives honed to razors. I had seen chief engineers and boiler monkeys before and I was not frightened, but these were particularly scorched and blackened, as if they had been living in a soot box or cinder bin. They could have just come up from hell itself and found the upper earth foul and disagreeable with its fresh air free of smoke and steam and fume.

I saw one thing. I saw John heap a plate with mule meat and send it to the wheelhouse with the darkened windows and welded hatches. I never saw the meat go but later I noticed that the plate on the catwalk had been licked clean.

I can't say whether the Idiot's wandering started off the looting and pillage. It was the noise the Idiot made that was the first alarm, the Idiot made a noise like a mule braying, and I say this because the Idiot's mule noise was so like a mule braying that for a moment, when they first heard it, John and his crew stopped in mid-chew to consider the slaughtered carcass head buzzing with flies beside them. I think the Idiot must have come into where the cratered lake people were gathered lunching on their pilings, and the Idiot wanted the figurine fetishes the people were shaking at him to keep him away. He would reach out for a cornhusk doll dressed to ward off the evil eye and a woman would shake the doll at the Idiot and then withdraw it as he approached. It was a game at first that went bad, when the Idiot stamped around in fury, turning around and around on his muddled head the cap bright with the pointed sheriff's star. I could see the red-rimmed drunkard considering a club to use on the Idiot but thinking better of using the snake stick we used to pin down the heads of the water moccasins when they crawled up the pilings from the creek. The red-rimmed drunkard stepped up and jabbed at the large Idiot with the stick that was forked with sharp ends, and the Idiot snatched it from him, and in a rage of mimicry poked it back at the red-rimmed drunkard, who may have met it partway in his usual stumbles. When he met the stick it was with his eyes and in a moment he was blind.

Now a club swung out from behind a plastic apron

and caught the Idiot upside his head. Now a lead stick bent across his shoulders in a swing a woman would make. Now some knives came up and sliced at the Idiot's arms as he hid his face, the Idiot letting off his awful bawl.

Lonny, the weeping man who said *Fuck,* and Ira Dench rushed the fray with pistols and an ax and pulled the Idiot out of the gobble squall and inflictions. They could not calm the Idiot and he threw them off with tremendous strength. *Goddamnit,* said Lonny, *all he wanted was just a toy on a string,* and he ripped the nearest fetish from a woman's neck and pressed it into the Idiot's bloody hands. The Idiot beheld his new toy as Ira Dench bent to the red-rimmed drunkard spinning and kicking on the ground, grinding his fists into the deflated spaces of his empty eye sockets.

Hope that never happens to me, said Ira Dench.

Careful, boys, shouted John, still hunkered by the picnic, *they're putting the evil eye and the whammy-jammy on you.*

And it was true, all around, the women were hissing and clucking and making invocations. They were seized with spitting fits, and they broke open seedpods and salted Lonny, Ira Dench, and the man who said *Fuck* with dirt and powders.

It put Lonny on a rage, and he swung his ax over

their heads and herded them into the cutting shed. *God-damnit*, I heard him say, *now give it up, give me all them toys*, and Ira Dench collected the fetishes first under shaky-handed pistol cover of the weeping man who said *Fuck*, then they stripped the people of their knives and then their clothes which they threw aboard the small dark ship by the bundle.

Now stay in here till we're done, won't no more bodies get hurt, Lonny said, Lonny and his crew backing out of the shed below me so close I could have leapt onto their shoulders.

I watched them go aboard their ship and then brace ladders across the rail to the dock as if to lay siege to the shore.

Don't forget to get the nets, John said to Lonny.

Lonny and the crew carried aboard sacks of oysters snatched from the dugouts, boxes of fresh fish from the shallow-draft schooner. They carried away cartons of fresh gourds and tuber fruit from my ruined garden, fresh hackberries gathered by the hatful. They took pots of paint aboard that the Idiot immediately stepped in, tracking color across the deck; they took light bulbs twisted from their sockets, boxes of tacks, and bundles of shingles; from the bottom of the creek they hoisted up the soda machine and took that too. Where they saw a mound of coal and a wheelbarrow to haul it, they took both. They laid hoses from the fishhouse pumps and filled their tanks: fresh water, fuel oil, and kerosene. And when there wasn't much else left to take, they pried open their aft hatches and the soft-skulled child, the one who I had built a step for so he could shuck and eat, the same one who had just been going down in my place to fetch cold sodas from the creek bottom for my nickels, the soft-skulled child showed them where to find the ice that he volunteered to go aboard and help them shovel. He was just about to go aboard and clean the 'tween-deck spaces with a rag on a stick when one of his mothers snatched him away and made him sit on the bus where Lonny was robbing the white-eyed driver of his clothes and a fishtooth comb.

Don't forget these nets, John said, pointing down into the shallow-draft schooner. *Fire up the boilers, Master Chief*, John said to Black Master Chief Harold and his boiler monkeys. John set foot on the schooner and broke off its mast and split a spar over his knee. He crossed the mast and spar and covered it with sail, cinching the corners with thick cord. For his new kite he tied strips of dress rags from the cratered lake women's clothing. He packed a flask of gasoline, some matches dipped in wax, and a coil of lanyard hemp. I watched John fold his kite into a long rolled package like a longbow and quiver that he strapped to his back with his wagon-rein belt. *Send these to the cleaners,* he said to Lonny, handing up the rough muleskin cloak and grunged white nightshirt.

Until that time I had been feeling less than useless to the man I had set myself to be like a tick upon. I was sure there was no way I could ever be useful to such a man, who needed convicts for crew, mule meat to eat, kites built from the rigging of ships. I was figuring no way for me to fetch in with such a man until I heard and saw he wanted his cleaning done, and I could do it, I could boil and scrub that nightshirt cleaner than white, scrape that mulehide soft with a clamshell, and work the ragged poncho into a proper cloak. I could do it, would do it, and I knew it would be done in the right way, not what Lonny had done with it, not by just running it up the mainmast to dry out crisp and hairy in the sun.

Now Fishboy would come down out of his nest. Hadn't it been me, the human-being boy, who'd helped bury the dead cook? Had swabbed his slippery spillage? Had brought gas and water in which to bathe? And wasn't it my cartonated encampment burnt down and my garden ruint and my work not to be done again at John's own hands? *Yes sir,* I thought as I readied myself to come down and sign on aboard, *I am on you like a tick.*

I was going to be on him like a tick until in a quick splash of time he disappeared. He had just been standing there naked with his kite package on his tattooed back. He had just been standing there holding Lonny and Ira Dench apart arguing over the mulehead, Lonny wanting to use it as bait on a rope for eels, Ira Dench wanting to split it open to make sweetbread. John settled the matter by picking up the mulehead and piking it in the bow of the ship, a furry figurehead dripping thickly into the creek. John considered the mulehead for a moment, checked his shoulder-slung parcel, and took a breath that seemed to last for several minutes. He took a breath so deep that I watched his back bellows out so that the tattoos there grew and grayed, and then John dove straight into the stain on the creek the dripping head had made. For as long as I could watch down the creek I did watch, and I never saw him surface.

Let's not forget John's nets, I heard Lonny say, *or we'll have to come all the way back for them.* I slunk back down in my nest wondering if I should go ahead and get aboard with Lonny and his crew, even knowing there had been something wrong with the way Lonny looked at me and talked to me as I scrubbed his back the first night with gasoline.

Lonny had let the cratered lake people file out to the bus, there being no call for finish fish that day. All the finish fish were stacked in boxes on the deck of the ship. Lonny and the weeping man who said *Fuck* stripped the nets from the dugouts and robbed the net house, hauling purse seines, bottom nets, stake nets, and drift nets. Any scrap of webbing with a line and cable on it they put aboard their ship.

Fishboy was the whisper.

It was close.

Fishboy was the whisper again.

It was real close. The bottom of my osprey hideout began to fill with blue fog, blue fog blowing up the drainpipe, blue fog creeping around my knees. I leaned over the nest's edge and looked down, and there she was, Big Miss Magine on her hands and knees, elephantine black and bare, Lonny having stripped her of her dropcloth floral sundress, her brown lips around the downspout of the drainpipe, blowing her blue breath up to me, then whispering

Fishboy? Where my finish fish, Fishboy?

She put her lips back around the drainspout and blew more blue fog up to me, then began to suck it out. I knew I wouldn't be sucked through the bottom of the osprey nest and through the pipe but I stepped around trying to step out of the fog, and I must have stepped on a weak place in the wattled wall, a place from which I had picked twigs to whittle.

The best about crashing out the bottom of the osprey nest was that the hole was small and fingered with sharp sticks that scraped my lice bites as I fell past them. I had never had an itching scratched so complete at once. I was in a scratched-itch ecstasy when I splatted deep in the valley of Big Miss Magine's black bare bosoms. She had caught me square and clapped her arms around me so that I was smothered and obliged to snorkel breaths that flubbered against her skin like a snore. Her own breathing was excited deep and rattly, and when she spoke, my ear pressed to her breast, it was the sound like when you hold your own ears and talk, except you would never say to yourself *You is mine, Fishboy, you is all mine.*

Help! I said, as I felt her carry me away, my arms pinned in her embrace, my legs a little free to kick her gut as hard as I was able.

Help! I said, and she had a coughy rattling laugh, phlegmy, and I wondered was this the source of blue fog, something dead in her lungs. Smothered as I was against her nakedness, I could not smell her breath, I could only smell fish oil in her sweat and the acrid smell of the bus tires the cratered lake people burned outside their houses at night to smoke away their mosquitoes.

The valley of her breasts was slick with my squirming and her fish-oil sweat and I slid up a little higher to get my head out of the skin. I turned my head around to see she was taking us into the empty cutting shed. Big

Miss Magine nuzzled me and bit into my only earlobe in a way I knew she was blood-hungry, beyond playful, bit in a way I was sure to be eaten alive.

The weeping man who said *Fuck* came into the cutting shed slopping gasoline across the floor. *Help!* I shouted to him, but I could see that to him I was just a small last finish fish some old nigger woman was about to stun with a lead stick in the darkness of just one more cutting shed he was set on to burn. *Help!* I yelled anyway, as anybody would.

Hush, Fishboy, I have you now, said Big Miss Magine and my head was rapped sharply, sharply, so that one of my eyes was knocked a little into orbit and the things I heard and saw went dreamy, the backfire of the purple bus leaving the lot, Lonny's shouts just outside to get ready to cast off, the way the small ship's smoke curled into the cutting shed and mixed in spirals with the flames that roamed the buildings and followed the trails of slopping gasoline.

Big Miss Magine stroked me down on the table, her thumb working into my neck as if to find a good gill place to put in the knife and jig out a fillet.

When I felt something sharp against my neck I beat and pushed her from me.

I beat and pushed with my fists, and in one of my fists was my butter-turned knife.

I pushed from Big Miss Magine with my butter-turned knife until I felt my fingers enter her skin and tick against her heart.

Her grip on my neck let go and I pitched off the cutting table, stepping into the slippery sluice. The ceiling of rolling smoke came lower as I clambered outside onto the dock. My eyes were unfocused and dreamy, one eye seeing the propeller-churned creek water brown and frothy, the other eye seeing how close the small ship's bow swung in its turn over my head so that my face was licked by the side-hung tongue of the figureheaded mule. I made a grab at a loop of bowline and saw that one of my arms was bloody to the elbow. I drew my arm back but it was as if the ship was repulsed by what it had seen. As it backed away into the creek I could see myself, the murderous Fishboy, reflected in the dark wheelhouse windows, a small figure framed by the rolling flames, all pumpkin orange and chiminey red.

Fishboy! roared the fire around me.

I tipped forward to the edge of the dock ahead of the fire spilling sizzling tar at my heels. The ship backed and backed across the creek into the other shore, its propeller cutting into the bank so that its stern climbed out of the water and began to break the low limbs of the shorelining trees. The stern beat against an old oak until from its crown dropped the two men in prison blues shackled at the wrists from their hiding place. They fell and rolled awkwardly onto the deck, on their pale frightened faces the set resignation of their addition to the ship's manifest.

Flames were up my back and I teetered. Clanking and clattering, shifting gears with a blast of boiler smoke, the small ship headed straight to me on the dock. It seemed to take so long that I wondered if I would get one more chance to pull myself aboard before the heat of the fire would shove me in the creek.

As I fanned my arms for balance and tried to focus my eyes I went dreamy again. I felt myself fall forward and bathe in coolness. Everything was quiet in my dream. In my dream I saw the bow of the ship splinter the last of the dock I was standing on, and the wheelhouse, shouldering the smashed burning timbers, break open its hatch. I was grabbed by the scruff of my neck and taken in a geography of embrace, sinewy muscles of arms like red clay banks along a river, boulders for teeth in a mouth set like a cave in a silver waterfall, eyes like the first evening stars at the end of the day, the end of a day when the fishhouse burned, the purple bus delivered naked people home, and a truant soft-skulled child sought shelter in the ruins of my cartonated encampment.

In this true dream the failing sky was lit by a small burning kite.

I was dead and drowned. I lay on the bottom of the fishhouse creek looking up at the night sky through a low tide. I could make out amber lights of stars and the moon dulled by the peat water of the creek. I was a carcass comfortable in the cool shifting underwater eddies. My bed must have been made of sluice spillage, what the shuckers and the filleters in the cutting shed gutted from the fish and seashells they cut, bowels and bladders for my pillow, ribbons of brain woven with strings of eyes for a blanket. Around me things seemed suspended in front of my badly focused eyes, inner organ things still alive, floating and falling, aborting, bursting and blinded, draping everything everywhere dying and foul.

And I was dead. And I was thinking how I must have died, and thinking of that I remembered the fishhouse fire and how my butter-turned knife went into Big Miss Magine until my fingers ticked against her heart. Thinking of that I thought I would hold my arm to my face to see if I could see it, being dead, and I stirred.

Having made murder I was not surprised when I heard a man's voice say *Fishboy.*

Knowing who that was, I thought to myself *Yes, Devil?*

It was like my bed shifted and my covers were thrown off, and for the first time I had the notion that for being dead underwater, my breath was not wet.

I'm going to set you down now, Fishboy, the man's voice said again. *Do you think you can stand up?*

My head rolled as the devil set me down, and I saw that what I thought were fish and seashell guts were red wet tendons and pink bones tipped in yellow fingernail, pulsing in little trembles, and I saw the arms were like clay bars in a river that ran out from a damp khaki shirt. I looked up and there were the long lengths of silver waterfall hair, the hair well brushed and clean, the hair hiding much of the face except the lower part, webs of muscle and fat lathered by the obvious tongue when the man spoke, the tongue slipping over the ivory edges of teeth, bright to the molars when he said *Don't be frightened, Fishboy, I'm not going to hurt you.*

Still, I backed away as anybody would, reaching behind me, now not sure if I was in the creek bottom dead or alive somewhere else, and my hands that reached behind me touched a spoked wheel taller than myself, and my eyes focused on the stars I had seen and the moon, and I saw that the stars were the little lights from an electric set of radios and compasses and boxes that could tell directions in an unremarkable sea, and the moon, the moon was the sun when you looked at the sun through dark smoked glass, like the dark smoked glass of John and Lonny's ship's wheelhouse, and that is where I was.

I heard them call you Fishboy around the dock, said the man turned inside out. *My name is Watt. I sometimes steer the ship but don't call me Captain.*

I shook my head no, I wouldn't.

You should stay up here in the wheelhouse until we pick up John this evening, said Mr. Watt. *We can then find something for you to do.*

I nodded my head yes.

Something small fluttered through the air over us and left oily marks on the inside of the smoked glass as it struck and burst against it.

Shoo out that sparrow before we get too far from shore, said Mr. Watt.

It was my first job aboard a ship. It was my first job being back alive.

I chased that bird around the wheelhouse under Mr. Watt's pedestaled captain's chair. I chased the bird across the electric boxes and through the tangle of wires that came out behind them. I chased that bird across the empty chart tubes to a dog-door hatch that led to the rest of the ship. The bird went out and I followed.

I followed the sparrow down a passageway past a stateroom strong with the smell of large animal skins — elk, deer, and horse.

Beyond the stateroom was a sealed hatch hot to the touch. I swung it open to a hot roar, and two steps led down to a floor of cumulus cloudbanks ripping with thunder and lightning. The tapered top of a ladder rose up from the middle of this place I figured to be the way down to the engine room.

I sealed the hatch and went down the passage shooing the sparrow along into the galley. I found the galley just as the crew had recently left it sacking for food. Broken cupboard doors opened and clapped shut. Condiment bottles rolled across the floor as the ship dipped and eased along. A crock of rancid butter and a jar of syrup were stuck to the table, the spoons the sailors had used to eat from them cemented wherever they had been tossed. The crude sink was more spittoon than washplace, and a tub of something rolled around with the fingerprints of each man who tasted of it for something edible other than what it actually was, lard. A large tin of spent grease had another record of its own, samples of several flying insect species collected from several ports of call along several coasts. Beside this the brown-and-black sparrow pecked at a bag of spilled rice.

I scooped up the sparrow and went to the aft cabin door which opened onto the deck. I opened the door and the air was bright and fresh, the sun strong on my face. I tossed the bird skyward but it fluttered back in fear and now beat around my face like a horsefly would. It finally lit on my head and nested itself in my hair.

Out on deck Lonny was running lifting lines down into the lazaret, the cargo storage in the stern, to bring up mounds and mountains of nets. Ira Dench and the weeping man who said *Fuck* were mending and weaving together the odd-fitting nets they had stolen at the fishhouse. I had never seen such mending and weaving, the way they used their teeth to hold and cut the twines, spreading the meshes between their knees and elbows. Near them on the main hatch sat the Idiot, safely out of the way, playing with a clutch of fetishes, his right foot stuck in a pot of red paint.

In the crease of the port rail the two men in prison blues were scattering tools from a toolbox, working at the shackles that held them together at the wrists. It was an exasperating huddle of cursing, dulling files, and breaking saws. As they did their work, they cut their eyes around them and muttered, secreting sharp punches and shanks of broken blades into their institutional boots.

In the stern quarter the sheriff's corpse sat tilted on a nail keg. The way his head leaned over the rail it appeared he was blissfully considering our wake.

Fishboy!

Slimy strong fingers pinched my neck skin and hefted me off my feet, the aft cabin door slamming and my feet cracking back and forth across the passageway walls as Mr. Watt took me back into the wheelhouse.

I told you to stay up here with me in the wheelhouse, he shouted at me, his apparent redness everywhere flushed and twisting. *You stay up here until John is aboard, and stay away from Lonny.*

He sat me roughly down in the bottom of a calendar clock case. Claws dug into my scalp as the sparrow fluffed itself down, hiding deeper in the nest of my hair.

Well, at least you got the bird out, he said, and I wondered about his eyes. Mr. Watt turned the wheel a spoke and put a looped line on it.

They follow us out, drink salt water, and die, he said. *At night sometimes we get a whole migrating flock attracted by our lights.*

I didn't mean to flinch when Mr. Watt stood over me, but I had never seen a man turned inside out before.

Get a good look at me, Fishboy, he said. I lay un-
flinching, rocking back and forth in the calendar clock
case, Mr. Watt telling me about a child turned inside out,
a child resting in the coolness of a potato bin, waiting for
its father and its brothers and its sisters to finish their
dinners and go to bed so that the child's appearance
would not shorten their appetites, and there was the
child, waiting in the coolness of the potato bin blackness,
sitting on the earthen floor, waiting for its mother to
lower the fire in the hearth and extinguish all the candles
except the one, and she, its mother, would take that one
candle down and coo the child out of the bin, the child
coming out slowly and sitting in its mother's lap, drinking thin gruel from a bowl, suckling the last of its baby
brethren's milk from its mother's breast, the mother
stroking the turned-inside-out child's hair with her own
fine brush, her family silver initial on its handle, gently
brushing the child's tufts and knots into a cascading silver veil, telling the child how beautifully its hair caught
the candlelight.

One night the child awoke from a dream crying out
because in its dream it had lost its silver hair, and the
child turned inside out wandered out crying into where
the family was eating. The brothers and the sisters top-
pled their crude stools, shouting and screaming, pushing

at their brother with a broom, pushing at him with a pike from the fire, with pieces of kindling. *Back, back, back into your hole,* the enraged father said, beating at the child with a dog whip and then slashing at the mother with it. *Bringing such an abomination into this world, demon bitch,* said the man as he beat the woman, beating her until she was quiet and seeping on the floor. The child fled back into the potato bin and turned tight circles in the dirt there as the bin doors were locked, then nailed with a shutter. In this way the child learned thirst.

A famine came across the land and everything anyone might eat in their houses they put into a pot of boiling water, and in his house, the inside-out child trembled in the potato bin just to smell the steam. His father and his sisters and his brothers added to their pot their last ingredients of food and boiled it down: an onion, a hide, seeds for the next planting season; and all throughout their house and all throughout their land there was not vermin nor insects nor tree bark nor soot scraped from the inside of cooking chimneys that had not been put into a boiling pot, and in this way the child's family learned hunger.

And it had been weeks since the shutter to the potato bin had been nailed and no sound issued forth, and the father and the brothers and the sisters took counsel, and they said *Why should we starve when that thing,* they said, pointing to the nailed-shut shutter, *when that thing fattens itself on our potatoes?*

Yes, said one of the brothers, *why should it have all of the potatoes and carrots while we have nothing?*

Yes, said one of the sisters, *it grows fat eating all of our potatoes and carrots and turnips while we starve to death!*

Yes, said the father, *the sound of it eating all of our food keeps me awake at night!*

So the ones with strength, that could, took up the pike from beside the fire, took up the hammer, and the rest clawed with their nails upon the shuttered door, and after a weak day and a night they broke away the shutter and opened the lock on the potato bin door. They leaned forward into the dark space, there was no light to see by, the candles boiled for tallow stew, and their eyes were not accustomed to such darkness and they were weak, and they were all too weak to fend off the child turned inside out, whose eyes were more capable than a cat's and whose strength had been nourished by sucking minerals from the mud of the bin bottom, and nourished by his largest memory, the memory of his mother leaking thickly on the floor. The child had enough sustenance to slay his father and to slay his brothers and to slay his sisters with the tendoned strength of his inside-out muscled hands. And finishing his work, he made a bonfire of the house and sat watching it burn from a hilltop. He sat watching it burn as he worked out the weeks of silver-haired tangles with his mother's fine initialed brush.

Mr. Watt turned the ship's wheel a spoke.

Get a good look at me, Fishboy, Mr. Watt whispered. *I, too, began as a boy.*

At about midnight Mr. Watt roused me from the calendar clock box and set me outside the wheelhouse hatch as if he were putting out the cat. He said they would be picking up John soon and for me to go aft and look useful, like I had been part of the crew all along, as John did not care for stowaways or children around Lonny.

I stood at the rail for a moment trying to rake the sparrow from my hair. I stood and considered the sky. I thought how wrong I had been thinking when I was dead lying on the creek bottom that I was looking at a night sky through low water. I had no doubt that I was now looking at the night sky at high tide. Even though there was no way to mark the high water, no jetsam thread along the shore, no rush of fresh surf up a beach, I was sure by the way it felt, standing there considering the billions of brightnesses, that the earth was swollen under the dark canopy of heaven and the ocean was lifting me among the stars.

Go on, Fishboy, said Mr. Watt, so I went along the dark rail to the aft deck.

In the edge of the decklight I startled Ira Dench who was taking a break from his mending and trying to summon a weather forecast in the weavings of his cat's cradles.

Boy, you gave me fright, he said. *You some kind of fish freak?* And I guessed it was my eyes, the way one looked one way and the other had its own looking-the-other-way flounder-like orbit. Maybe it was the fish-lipped pinchedness of my face, or the way I hid my bloody arm behind me, the crook of my elbow dorsal finning my back.

I shook my head no, and he went back to casting with his string, picking up loops with his fingers, cursing when he dropped one.

Calm seas for two days, humidity all right, barometer on a slight fall, said Ira, reading the string. *Thunderstorms later in the week, nothing serious, part of a front moving through. Thunder makes Lonny jumpy, is all.* Ira spread his knuckles for me to see the hemp image and I thought I saw what looked like a white embroidery of a thunderbolt in his weave, like those on the caps and collars of sailors who sometimes passed through the fish-house from the north.

Now let me give you some fortune, said Ira Dench and he wound the string across the backs of his hands and bit loops that he draped on his thumbs.

Not so good, Fishfreak, he said. He wound the string and folded it into his pocket.

He said, *If I was to give you a good head-start throw overboard, do you think you could make it to that shoreline?* He pointed to a sawtooth profile of pinpointed lights, a skyline we were passing. I had never been to a city, and to see a city from the sea puts your mind against it. I stared at it unconvinced, the thin mirage of brilliance so easily doused by the smallest wave rushing toward it.

Do you think you could swim that far if I was to give you a good throw? he said.

I looked at the tiny skyline. I looked at Ira Dench. I looked at the soda machine the crew had stolen from the bottom of the fishhouse creek. Already the men in prison blues had worked on its change box with their files and saws and the soda machine lay ruptured against a hatch. I looked at the soda machine and realized it had always been the distance limit of my swimming.

I didn't say anything, and Ira Dench said to decide soon before we got too far out to sea. Then he said he had two words of advice for me.

Rogue wave, he said.

Ira Dench said every time he spun the string around there was a rogue wave knot coming into the corner of my fortune.

At first I wondered if him wanting to throw me over was more for his good luck or for mine, him not wanting to be aboard the same ship as someone prone to a rogue wave. And then I wondered just as he could see forward, I wondered just how far he could see back, back a day or so to a boy with his butter-turned knife elbow-deep in a black woman's bosom.

I had the feeling there was more that he was going to say to me when he spotted a pole Lonny had fetched aboard that was thick with cratered lake people's shoes strung by their laces, and Ira Dench began stripping the laces out saying *Never underestimate native laces like these handmade with hemp, puts a kind of voodoo on the item if you believe in that type of thing.*

It was easy to skulk and dodge around on the deck because of the mountains of net Lonny had pulled from the lazaret. I had once seen a mile of pound net and judging from what I could figure here, there was about a hundred miles of net in piles that I could hide around until the right moment. The white decklights cast everyone's face bright and pale, Lonny and the weeping man who said *Fuck* trying to bring down a steel net bar that had fouled in the rigging overhead, the Idiot still playing with his fetishes on the main hatch, the two men in prison blues roughing up the sheriff's corpse. Still shackled, one would give the corpse a right-fisted punch in the face and then the other could apply a left-fisted punch, and in between, the sheriff's nose shifted back and forth from cheek to cheek like a movable festering boil.

Big Miss Magine's bloodstain was starting to wear off my arm, but in the bright decklight it showed plain in the creases of my wrist and knuckles, and it gave my fingernails a look that if you had ever seen human blood dried on someone's hand, you would have known I had plenty of it dried on mine. A sea hose was running cold salt water by a scupper and I knelt there pulling off my shirt to scrub with. It was a good scrub for the shirt as well, still steeped with the cook's spillage. The stains on my flesh were stubborn and resistant to salt water and spit and the scrubbing of my rough shirt, and the way the rocking ship cast its decklight and lanterns around, what sometimes I thought was stain was just shadow, and sometimes the shadow seeped deeper within my skin.

I had just finished as much as I could do when the sparrow fluttered from my hair and began to sip at the seawater running from the hose. The bird was dull-eyed and slow from drinking the salty water and was easy to catch, so I caught it and flung it over the rail toward where only about three pinpricks of light were left on the shoreline. Our decklights and lanterns, and even a star or two above, were brighter, and I watched the sparrow do a weak turn and light itself on the hatch near the Idiot.

The Idiot had already broken apart most of his cornhusk and rag-stick fetishes, and when he caught sight of the sparrow he let out a little jackass bray and crawled toward the bird, the pot-stuck foot clunking across the hatch cover.

Stay and play nicely, goddamn you, I heard Lonny say to the Idiot as Lonny worked the lifting lines to free the net bar hung in the rigging. The Idiot still made for the sparrow and I felt bad for the bird and angry with it at the same time. I figured to go fetch it and give it one more toss toward shore and then be done with it. I was doing more to save it than it was to save itself.

I put on my wet shirt and then made myself invisible in the way that you can, my head turned down, my eyes on my pinched-toe feet making careful quick steps across the deck, leaning into the walls of net and ducking now and then. I was almost to the hatch when a fireball came roaring out of heaven and struck me down squarely. I scrambled up and the divine fire spun down and laid me out again, and I was sure if I had not just wet my shirt I would have been set ablaze.

I heard it hovering overhead again, and in cringing

anticipation I looked over my shoulder at the thing, and it was in its final glory, its flames devouring the gasoline-soaked strips of black women's clothes with the click and pop of lice and ticks, then the mainsheet sail went red onto the crossed sticks that sputtered in colors of bruise and infection.

John hailed us from the skirt of a sea buoy, a round nun kind meant to ring, but the bell looked broken by some ship's passing cannon practice and its habit was pockmarked and rife with rifleshots and seabird splatter. John coiled his kite's line around his flexed arm and flung it aboard, leaping the rail himself as we passed near. In the white decklight I could see John's hair and beard were a tangle of seaweed, broken fishing line, and old anchor chains. Mr. Watt straightened our rudder and beneath a fresh plume of exhaust that showered us with cinders our ship tossed the buoy in its wake. Moored to the floor, the clapper snapping in the jagged shards of its bell, the buoy leaned after us like a watchdog straining at its chain.

My ears is clogged, said John, bouncing his head.

I can't help you yet, said Lonny, *I got to hold this line until we can put a whip line on that net bar.* The weeping man who said *Fuck* was climbing up a net wing that Lonny held fast by the winch.

What? said John.

I said GET YOUR OWN GODDAMN EAR-DROPS OUT OF THE GEAR SHED! said Lonny.

I saw that John could not hear Lonny, and I saw the gear shed and I thought that if I could find the ear-drops I would be on my way to becoming useful.

In the shed a fire extinguisher was all the eardrops could be and I took it over to John still trying to pass off a little invisibility. John pumped the canister while looking at me and then squirted some of the stuff in his ears. The stuff smelled like laundry soap cut with paint thinner. A clump of fungus fell from one ear and a mollusk from the other.

Where's this child come from, Lonny? John said. *Is it one of yours?*

Lonny leaned back from the winch still holding the wing net line and said *What child? That child? That ain't one of mine unless it wants to be.*

Fetch me that sea hose, John said to me and I jumped to it and held it as he washed, the thick gray mud from the ocean floor flushing away, revealing the mazes of tattooed cartographies on his arms, chest, and back, the sea island atolls shifting and mountain peaks lifting as he bent to scrub his legs. There was a fresh shark strike on one calf; the other one I had first noticed in my gourd garden already healing, several cartilage teeth still embedded and molded over with a thin veneer of skin.

Can you work net? John said to me. *Can you mend meshes and haul in the lines? Can you run a winch without killing somebody?*

I looked down at my pinched-toed feet and balled up my fists in the front of my shirt. I did not know how to do those things.

Hey, said Lonny, *can he cook? We're all about to starve to death.*

Can you cook? John asked me and I remembered the warning about cooking the last cook had told me just before he died. I shook my head no. I could not cook.

Well, son, said John. *I think you have two choices. I think you can either cook or you can swim.* When John said that, I turned and looked for what was left of the bright pinpointed skyline, but it had dulled and disappeared. There was nothing to swim to, nowhere to swim for, nothing out beyond our ship but the stars and the white wake hissing behind us.

So I nodded okay and Lonny said *And some biscuits, make me a whole basket of biscuits. I'm real hungry. And gravy. Biscuits and gravy. And fried steak with a chicken crust, maybe some mashed potatoes. Stew up some collard greens and tomatoes with brown sugar, I could go for that.*

I drug myself along to the aft cabin door that led to the galley. *Hey,* Lonny said, *also don't forget my eggs. I*

always like to have a side of eggs, and don't make them
greasy, I can't abide greasy eggs, you hear me?

I heard him as I drug myself along, hearing everything he asked for taking piece after piece of hope from me of ever getting through my life not split in two with an ax.

*I*n the galley was a pot big enough for me to swim in. I put it on the stove and filled it bucket by bucket from the spittoon sink. I put the flame to it. I guess the men in prison blues had ransacked the big blade board, it was full of empty outlines where knives and cleavers should have gone, and when I took a pan out on the deck to gather some fish and tuber fruit for finish fish stew, the prison men fairly clanked with cutlery when they moved. John had come in to rest on his carpet of hides so the men in prison blues had begun to amuse themselves by knocking off the Idiot's cap and then kicking him in the seat of his pants when he bent over to pick it up. Shackled as they were, it took certain steps to do this, and they managed it as if they were dancing a reel.

All the nets lay over the litter of our departure and John had been right, I was not strong enough to move them around, so I picked at the edges. The fish were mixed up in the stuff the crew had stolen, there were tacks everywhere and shards from the wooden box of light bulbs that tinkled into glass against themselves as the ship pitched and rolled. Vegetables and gourds from my garden were on the verge of garbage, starting to smell along with the oysters and shellcut that all needed to be iced down in the hold, perishables starting to perish because the person whose job it was to tend them had recently been split in two with an ax.

I tried to get at the ice in the hold by prying up the deckplate with a shovel but I broke the handle and when no one was looking I threw it overboard.

I stood on the stove and stirred the finish fish stew with a spoon the size of a boat paddle. The stew had several good-sized whole fish in it, more parts left on them than I ever got at the fishhouse, and short of a knife to slice the gourds and tuber fruit, I stomped on them to make them tender if I couldn't make them sweet. Standing there stirring the stew and waiting for mealtime I felt some hope return even if there weren't any biscuits.

I had opened the dry goods locker to fetch some biscuit mix and had found a large rat guarding the flour. *Fuck off*, said the rat, the rat picking spittle dough from his teeth with the tip of his tail. *Fuck off, go away*, he said, and I did.

This stew puts an edge on my ax! said Lonny, spitting out a mouthful across the galley table.

Now I remember where I saw you first, said John, spitting his spoonful out too.

It's not so bad if you just stick to the big chunks, said Ira Dench.

The men in prison blues, trying to work out eating shackled at the wrists, had not sampled theirs yet. It was clear the Idiot would eat anything put in a bowl before him. I figured only the man who wept and said *Fuck* would not eat at all, him being in a state of pain and shock, dripping sweat from just losing a toe.

Just before mealtime the Idiot had spotted that damn sparrow again and set off after the thing. I had already decided that the only way to draw the sparrow away from the ship lights and to the vague shore was to become a sparrow myself and I could not do that, I was sure, especially having to cook. The Idiot had spotted the half-dead bird hop and flutter back to my head-nest and the Idiot went lunging across the deck clumping, his foot still caught in the paint, stepping into Lonny holding the lifting line against the winch and kicking the lifting line out of Lonny's hand.

Lonny said he had once seen a winchman's arm ripped from the socket when the winchman tried to grab at a runaway line.

There must have been a moment when the weeping man who said *Fuck* heard Lonny curse the Idiot, saw the snaking rigging, could feel the loss of tension in the wall of rope and woven steel netting he was climbing to unfoul the ton-weight net bar above him. It was a moment for him to leap and fall from a great height or cling and be crushed, and what he did had been decided before he was born, when his mother still carried him in her womb, Lonny said, and she had been nearly struck down on a sidewalk by a falling steeplejack from a church spire, the sight of the steeplejack pleading up to her from the pavement with his hips sprouting from his neck had caused her to faint and go into labor, and she gave birth alongside the burst man to an undersized infant, the baby this man who wept and said *Fuck* began as, who now embraced the falling sheets of net and closed his eyes.

He had been lucky, only a corner of the heavy bar had come down near him, just its tip, and the tip came down squarely on the poor man's boot, the pressure squeezing the blood from his foot into his face, the face a red curdle as his throat opened and out of his mouth came his word.

FUCK!!! he had said.

Lonny chased the Idiot with an ax topside and when the Idiot hid in the lifeboat and pulled the shroud over his head Lonny broke open the turnbuckles, unfastened the lashings, and turned the crank handle that would ship the lifeboat over the side into the dark sea.

Lonny! said John, roused up by the ruckus, *We're short of crew as it is.* John cauterized the nasty gap in the man's toeline with a coal he took from a small metal box used to burn fragrant woods. He was delicate about it even as the men had to hold the man down, John not wishing to cut the man with his razor-sharpened fingernails as he performed the operation.

John shook the pinched-off gnarly-nailed toe out of the boot and knotted it on a fetish string that he hung around the Idiot's neck. John said maybe that would remind the Idiot to be more careful of where he stepped. He pulled the pot of paint from the Idiot's foot. It was red paint and the Idiot's bare foot and trouser cuff were brilliant with it.

I hope the bastard chokes on a bone, said Lonny at the table, and the way the men in prison blues were slipping fishbones into the Idiot's soup, that seemed likely.

The steel door to the engine room blew its bolts and out of the issuing smoke coalesced Black Master Chief

Harold, radiant black with sweat like fresh-chiseled coal, his chin streaked and gooed from fuel-tasting, his asbestos jacket smoldering. Behind him were his fire lackey and his boiler monkey, hints of fume from their nostrils, them not much larger than myself, their bent helmets hardly protecting their hair in the places where it was singed to broiled nubbles. They looked shot from cannons.

I had forgotten to send their meal buckets down so I opened the wicker basket trimmed with red-and-white checks to serve them on the china the crew had eaten the mule meat off of, but Lonny said *Put that away, that's just for meals ashore.* It really didn't matter because after the engine room trio sniffed at the finish fish stew bubbling on the stove they foraged for themselves in the lockers and found a jug of vinegar and a piece of something that I had also found and could not tell if at one time it had been a melon rind or a piece of rotten rubber trim like off a refrigerator. They passed around the vinegar and took a few bites from the refrigerator thing and eyeballed us, sniffing as if they found either us or fresh air foul and disagreeable.

Hey! said Lonny. *How come we didn't get any of that whatever-it-is stuff?* and Lonny set to cursing me, promising to whetstone his axes promptly.

While we are all gathered here together I want ev-

eryone to sign the ship's log, said John. He had an old book bound with the hide from a palomino pony. The book was passed around and men made marks in it. I did not know how to spell my name but I stood ready to make my mark. It did not matter. John passed the log around, and the log passed back and forth over my birded head but never did it reach my hands. I turned away when John began to read the new marks from the book of men.

X! said John.

Here, said Lonny.

X! said John.

Here, said Ira Dench. *Goddamnit,* he added, pulling off his fortune string and webbing it on again.

X! said John.

Fuck! spit out the man who said that, his foot paining him.

XX! said John and the men in prison blues held up their shackled wrists.

Triple X! said John and Black Master Chief Harold took his boiler monkey and fire lackey below.

Get up steam, said John after them, *we want to set the nets at daybreak.*

This last signature is illegible, said John. *There are severe penalties for poor penmanship.* He studied the signature, one eye closed.

O! he said.

O? said Lonny.

No, X! said John, motioning to the Idiot.

I'll sign for the sheriff, invoking power of attorney and all that, said John, making a mark and closing the book.

John said *If any come aboard and hate not his father and his mother and his wife and his children and his brothers and his sisters, and his own life too, he can not be a shipmate serving on this ship.*

I hate anything, Lonny said, and the crew was dismissed.

I took a cup of finish fish stew forward, my heart beating hotly in the darkness of the passageway.

I was coming to understand that Mr. Watt was a prisoner of the wheelhouse, a place kept cool by frigid air fans and darkened in the day by the smoked glass windows. Nighttime was daytime for Mr. Watt, when he could open the portholes and cross-ventilate the place, take off his thick khaki shirt and trousers he wore to protect his flesh from the sun that filtered in, hang the khaki to dry from the oozings of his muscles the day long.

When I came into the wheelhouse through the dog hatch my eyes weren't quite adjusted to the dark, and Mr. Watt was in pieces, his shirt hung on a porthole screw, his pants draping the captain's chair, and Mr. Watt himself leaning on the wheel in a way that all I could see was his disembodied floating head shrouded in silver hair. When he turned to me to take the cup of stew and I could see him without his clothes I was wishing my eyes were a little more nightblinded, because Mr. Watt was chewing a piece of hardtack, and with his shirt off you could see a section of blue tunnel-like muscle squirm up his throat to the back of his mouth to feed there from the bits of hardtack ground by the clattering teeth and corraled by the obvious tongue. I handed up my cup of stew and I couldn't tell if Mr. Watt was smiling at me or if everyone's jaw muscles run under our cheeks and hook behind our ears like spectacles.

Thank you, Fishboy, he said.

Mr. Watt lifted the cup to his mouth and sipped, and barely had a little trickle of my finish fish stew gone down his throat when his whole gut heaved to stop it, his gut squeezing the stew upward, drizzling through the side teeth and canines.

That's . . . that's delicious stew, Fishboy, Mr. Watt said, *and I think I'll save mine for later.* He set down the cup on the bridge and took up his hardtack again.

The men in prison blues had put a bone in the Idiot's bowl that the Idiot could not swallow, and now we could hear him braying and choking, and we could hear Lonny say how he could not stand hawking noises at the table when he was trying to eat.

You better go back to the galley and clean up, Mr. Watt said. *Try to make yourself useful to John, find something you can do. Can you tell him a story?* and I shook my head no. I didn't know any stories, I hardly knew my own.

I wanted Mr. Watt to know I had not been allowed to sign the log, so I asked him how my name was spelled, just in case. He said my name was spelled F-I-S-H-B-O-Y. I listened as hard as I could and understood it sounded like IF I JUST ACHE, BEER OR WINE.

In the galley the only person left was the Idiot, the Idiot making the horrible hawking noises and tearing at his throat, thrashing around and kicking. I saw the men had left in a hurry, their empty bowls on the table, one of Ira Dench's fortune strings, the palomino-bound ship's log. I climbed up on the stove and looked inside the pot. For all their complaining they had finished the stew, leaving some carcass heads and broken tuber rinds stuck to the pot's bottom. I pulled out the spoon like a boat paddle and went over to the Idiot red and frothing on the floor. I shoved the spoon into his mouth and reached down his throat. I had done this once before for a stray dog at the fishhouse and had gotten bitten for my thanks. I pulled a thick piece of fish spine from where it was wedged, in the Idiot's gullet, the bone edges pink where they had begun to cut, and made sure the spoon was free before I stepped back and cleared the table. I put the bowls in the spittoon sink, collected the piles of fishbones, and wiped the eating places with a wet rag. I shoved the ship's log that I had not been allowed to sign so roughly to the end of the table so that it struck the wall.

The Idiot lay on his back hawking softly once or twice before he got up and sat at the table. He sat there braying stupidly and blubbering until I made sure no one was looking and I gave him a sound broadstroke on the side of his head with my boat-paddle spoon. That seemed to shut him up so I could think, and I climbed down inside the stew pot which was littered with beautiful carcasses. I piled a few up against the side to sit on and fed myself from the little gutter running around the pot's bottom.

In a while I heard the Idiot shuffle out and I heard

someone come in and prop open the dog hatch. It was John. I could hear him talking with Mr. Watt. He wanted Mr. Watt to read the chart that ran over his shoulder and up his neck, but Mr. Watt said his eyes were worse than ever. Mr. Watt said by dead reckoning he figured they were pretty much in the same area where they left off dragging John's net the last time.

How many of us are there this trip? said Mr. Watt and I heard John come back in the galley to fetch the log. *Goddamnit, look at what that little cook has done to the log!* and I thought maybe I had roughed it up a little sliding it across the table. I didn't know at the time that the Idiot had been sitting there while I was eating, marking up hundreds of pages of X's with Idiot scrawl.

There's twelve of us counting the Idiot and the sheriff, said John. When Mr. Watt said why wasn't the Fishboy signed on, John said because he wasn't sure he wanted me aboard.

He can't work the nets, he can't cook, Lonny's already after him, and Ira thinks he's bad luck, like some rogue wave magnet, said John. *And now look what he's done to the log because I didn't let him sign on right away.*

Maybe you're right, said Mr. Watt.

I'm going for a swim, said John and I heard him pass through the galley and out the aft cabin door.

I sat in the bottom of the cooking pot, picking at the last of the best batch of finish fish stew I had ever made, but what my trembling hands could put to my mouth didn't seem to have much flavor, and failed to give me strength.

*O*n the aft deck the men slept in the piles of net, their bellies full from what I fed them. John had jumped the rail and was swimming below us in the deep somewhere. In the last hours of night a curtain of black rain swept us and the men turned on their stomachs in the ash-laden downpour. Around the stern, ballast stones from the hull of a sailing ship popped out of the black waves and rolled around, and I dodged one to look over the rail, and I saw John bringing them up by the armful and throwing them onto the ship.

There's my little vandal, John said to me when he climbed aboard. I still didn't know the Idiot had ruined his logbook. I thought he meant that I had bruised the book by shoving it across the galley table. I hung my head and helped him collect the ballast stones in a pile.

The circle of stones gave off a faint light, and I thought St. Elmo's fire or phosphorus fog. Out of the dull light two faint figures took shape, two men in gray rags putting out their hands as if to get warmth from the bluish lit stones.

No you don't, you don't run, Vandalboy, said John. He had me by the arm as I backed away from the odd conjuring going on. He said he wanted me to meet some friends of his from the *Thomas Hyde,* the ship whose stones he had fetched for this.

John, said one of the figures. *I should have known it was you.*

Hello Eiphey, said John. *Who's that with you?* and Eiphey said it was Oliver Griggs, the second mate.

John, said Oliver Griggs, and John said *Mr. Griggs.*

Eiphey asked John if John was still fishing with Mr. Watt, and John said if you could call a crew of criminals, mutants, idiots, freaks, and murderers a fishing crew, then he probably was.

Just like the old days, said Eiphey, and John said he guessed so.

Everybody considered the pale fire coming off the stones.

So how is Mr. Watt? said Eiphey, and John said he thought Mr. Watt's eyes were giving out, that it was getting nearly impossible for him to read the charts.

A small rough sea from the squall struck the ship

and the ballast stones shifted so that the gray figures flickered and became even fainter for a moment.

I guess you're wondering about your girlfriend, Eiphey said, and John said he was hoping maybe Eiphey had heard something from, well, down there.

Eiphey told him there was nothing new. He said *You still hear the shark story now and then but really nothing else.* He said *Sorry.*

It's all right, said John, *I have all the time in the world to keep looking.* John said he had just gotten more nets to help him look and that Black Master Chief Harold was working on a new engine to pull an even bigger net.

I heard something, said Oliver Griggs.

You, Mr. Griggs? said John.

Don't tell it, said Eiphey.

What do you mean, don't tell it? said John, and Eiphey said he only meant for Oliver Griggs to tell it if he was sure it was a true thing he was telling. *No offense, Oliver,* said Eiphey.

I know what you're saying, Eiphey Deacon, said Oliver Griggs. *I know what your meaning is: can a mutineer speak the truth, right? Well, to hell with you.*

That's not what I meant, said Eiphey.

Sure it is, said Oliver Griggs.

Tell it, said John.

What difference would it make? said Oliver Griggs. *Do you think I'm worried about being caught in a lie? What can be done to me that hasn't been done? Already my soul just stones scattered on the ocean floor. I'm not afraid of you anymore, Eiphey Deacon, or you either, John, so fucking big. Throw my stones back over the side, just don't insult me.*

Speak, said John.

Don't get your hopes up, John, said Eiphey Deacon. *It's a grim story I've heard several ways. Oliver's version we got from a man we found hugging a cask adrift the Horn. He was delirious.*

Tell it, damn you both, said John.

I won't be insulted, said Oliver Griggs.

Throw his stones over, Fishboy, John said.

You won't do it, thinking I might know something, said Oliver Griggs.

Over the side, Fishboy, said John. *Breathe your last free air ever, Oliver Griggs,* said John.

I had never seen angry ghosts argue and I was eager to put their stones over, but even as John told me to do it he never let go of my wrist. John himself pitched a ballast stone over the side. Oliver Griggs flickered for a moment and said *Wait.*

This is all I know, he said.

Tell it, said John.

Tell it, said Eiphey Deacon quietly, looking down at this campfire of the dead.

What I heard, said Oliver Griggs, *is that your wife or girl or whatever she was was found nearly drownt in a fisherman's net.*

Where? said John.

Be calm, said Oliver Griggs. *I think it was on that island where those wide stone steps go down forty or fifty feet to the heap of broken wine jars. Remember that trip? Wasn't that you? The sea was dark with wine for two tides. It was a long time ago but I thought it was you.*

Show me where, said John, and he uncovered a charted shoulder and leaned into the circle of misting stones.

God, John, I don't know, I can't read your awful flesh, said Oliver Griggs.

Show me, said John.

Try and show him, said Eiphey Deacon, and Oliver Griggs wafted around John in the blue light, prodding here and there with a finger that made John shiver.

Your touch is cold, said John.

Yours will be soon enough, said Oliver Griggs. *Maybe here,* he said, and he pointed to what looked like a pimple and John said not to toy with him, that there was no wrecked ship there.

Then maybe here, said Oliver Griggs, and he traced

a small island north of John's right kneecap. *I think this is where*, he said.

John squatted and studied the atoll tattooed on his knee, rubbing away some grime with spittle. *I haven't looked there in years*, he said.

I think that's where, said Oliver Griggs. *All I heard is that she came up almost drownt in some fisherman's net.*

Did he release her? John said.

What I heard is that they had like a school, like a university in the city, and at the university they had an aquarium. That's what I heard, I heard they put her in the aquarium.

John said we could make the island in a week.

There's more, said Eiphey Deacon. *Tell him the rest*, he said to Oliver Griggs.

Well, they had themselves a little civil war, the island was sieged and the town occupied. The animals in the zoo were butchered. They put embers in the eyes of people who could read. They were sacking the university when the government's white fleet sailed into the harbor. The university was saved and the aquarium spared, but not your wife or whatever.

What do you mean? said John.

A white ship's crew was garrisoned in the aquarium.

In the celebration of liberation they shot up the tanks and flooded the place.

No! said John.

Yes, yes! said Oliver Griggs, smiling. *Yes, you self-righteous son of a bitch. We took your flipping wife and gutted her and cooked her over little charcoal fires on the beach. It was a great party!*

NO! said John.

YES! said Oliver Griggs. *With a little red wine marinade she was delicious.*

John swung his fillet-sharpened fingernails through the blue vapor and Oliver Griggs diffused in two and laughed.

Yes, we also made her perform for her life and then we had her, and then we made some beautiful fillets. She was really something to look at except for her teeth. She had these canine teeth, said Oliver Griggs to Eiphey Deacon. *We made her bark like a seal while we threw her fish. It was just her teeth though. She had teeth like a common dog. A real bitch's mouth, if you know what I mean.*

John began to heave the ballast stones over the side in splashing volleys as Oliver Griggs laughed and Eiphey Deacon pleaded and then said farewell. In his frenzy to rid the ship of the stones John picked me up when I was holding one to help, and I was certain for a moment he would throw me over too, a worthless vandal who had heard what was breaking his heart, and I wished I had never heard it, and I thought that if he threw me over, I would cling to the stone and follow it to the bottom. I had been dead once before and it had not been so bad.

Go drop that stone in the hold, John said to me, calming. He said Mr. Watt had a collection of them to build a house with one day when he retired.

And when you come back, rouse the crew. It's almost light, time to set out the net.

I went away about to burst hauling the heavy stone, but the effort took my eyes away from seeing John sitting slumped on the hatch, his kneecap atolls caressed by the waves that fell from his face.

*T*he black rain lay so thickly on the sea that at dawn the sun could not find its reflection in the dull obscurant ink. Into the ink the men cast John's net with pitchforks and long poles, tamping the meshes and woven chafes into the dark water as if to dye the net black instead of letting it soak and sink to the bottom. When enough of John's careful snare had been pitched, pushed, and hauled hand-over-shackled-hand overboard, Lonny dropped the spreaders. The spreaders caught the water and the net opened in the ocean behind us as our ship began pulling its aft out from beneath the mountains of netting still on deck. We all worked our way forward, away from where the thick rolls of diamondback meshing slithered quickly over the side like sea serpents, away from where the coiled lines struck and snatched at your feet to drag you to a drowning deep and quick.

On this ship, where it did not matter if I could shuck one hundred and seventy-seven bushels of shell cut in six hours, I stayed close to John. I worked hard around him, spooling net needles, spreading my arms like a repair loom when he needed to stitch together a torn mesh. I watched him watch the deck empty itself of his net, I watched him chew the bottom of his beard, bouncing his hand on the cable that Lonny let roll from the winch drums. Lonny tried to slow the net's release with the foot brake but the bearings smoked and you could hear the brake shoes squeal and bind, failing against the pull of so much weight. Lonny protested that we were putting out too much net and he spit in the sea to prove it, Lonny's spittle a little froth string that sidled alongside us, almost dead in the water before it strung itself to our hull.

We've got no speed, Lonny said, and I could feel the ship slow beneath the drag, the bow rising as we shuddered to a stop even as our smokestacks brewed thick exhaust into the morning sky.

Go tell the master chief, John said to me, his thick cud of beard flopping to his chest. *Go tell the master chief more power, and hurry it up,* he said.

Like I said, I had never been to a city but I thought the engine room must be like one. I rag-wrapped the hatch handle against the heat to open it, and I was rushed by the roar of motors and sirens and fumes, rushed by a scorching heat that filled the hollows of my body so that I began to bake from the inside out. The searing blast stung my eyes and blew the damned sparrow from its nest in my hair. I reached once above me to snatch at the bird like someone might reach back to snatch at a hat that is blown while riding a galloping horse, but my errand was the most urgent kind, the redemptive kind, and I pulled myself along the passage with one thought in mind, to tell the master chief more power, more power for John to pull his precious net.

A ladder spired up through the neck-high cumulus of fume and I felt around with my feet for the rungs before climbing down. I descended from the cloudbank and ran down a boulevard of boilers, taking a side street by the electrical plant. Off the side street I took a shortcut through an alley where there looked like a brawl, piston arms pumping punches into cylinder blocks lying prone on the sidewalk, a ruptured gasket bleeding spent oil into a gutter.

I slowed my pinched-toe run on a footbridge that spanned a canal. In the canal spun the silver main drive shaft like a river of mercury flowing between mudbanks of grease. I slowed because for only the second time since we had left the fishhouse did I feel that Big Miss Magine had stowed away aboard the ship and was laying in wait for me somewhere. The first time was when I had been sleeping in Mr. Watt's empty calendar clock box. I was asleep, slipping into a dream, and the back-and-forth rocking of the ship seemed to me the way the purple bus rocked back and forth when Big Miss Magine stepped and climbed aboard. It startled me awake and sitting up seeing Mr. Watt's silver-veiled head floating in the captain's chair, I knew it had just been one of those tricks of sleep. But this time I was awake and the feeling was different, I felt she was close, I felt she was hiding in the engine room somewhere waiting for me. I kept turning to see her face gape from oily filters, her form in hunkered cowlings, her fingers flailing in ragged ropes fluttering from exhausts. In the fish oil sloshing hot in the bilge and in the burning rubber gaskets I smelled her skin and I smelled breath.

I kept to the main street, looking over my shoulder for footfalls the roar of the place made me deaf to.

I passed the salvage yard, the piles of accumulated wreckage dredged up in John's net, wreckage scavenged from maritime graveyards, heaps of any machinery John thought Black Master Chief Harold could use to build an ark engine, a motor that ran on brilliant particles, a motor John had only heard about third-hand, a motor that could run forever and pull an infinite amount of net, a motor that the master chief was consigned to construct with only pages torn from books and hearsay to help him.

I found Black Master Chief Harold and his fire lackey and boiler devil arguing at the construction site. They were huddled in the frame of the ark engine, their tools within reach around them, levered lengths of chain spanning the workspace, dirty work rags dried stiff and hanging above them like icicles of filth. They were arguing in the hand symbols men use when confusion and machinery drown language, when tossed thumbs mean to lift tons and jigged wrists signify *We could all be crushed.* Fingers punched asbestos-vested breastbones to punctuate a point, and fists of oven-mitt gloves wiped clean the blueprints that had been drawn in the air.

In a place like this, among men where my whistling lisp could never be mocked, I stood mute with my message from John. *More power!*

Tugging on the master chief's oil-soaked sleeve I

tried in my best hand-twisting monkey talk to explain the size of the net John had set out, how the ship was stalled in the water, how what was needed was more power, but the master chief brushed me aside and made a pipe-fitting motion with a fist butting the heel of his glove, which the boiler devil responded to by throwing a wrench across the floor in disgust.

I turned to the fire lackey with my message, pulling him to the coal bunkers that spilled around the mouth of the red-grated furnaces. I drew a shovel from the mound of coal and made a motion as if to feed the fires, but the fire lackey took the shovel from me and pointed to a color guard of gauges, the needle noses in their faces pegging red, and I understood that there was no more power, no more gain to be gotten, the engines were so stoked that the rivets used to hold the boilers together were occasionally popping off and stinging us where they struck us like wasps.

All I wanted was just a little more power for John's net, even just a little extra puff of black smoke from our stack to show I had completed my errand, and when the fire lackey left me to finish his argument with the master chief and the boiler devil, I took up the coal shovel again and turned the bolt on the furnace grate. The door swung open and there she was, there was Big Miss Magine, her big black face laughing in the fiery coals, laughing and hissing in the draft of the open door, *FISH*-hissing, *BOY*-roaring, the rushing air stoking her arms, her arms reaching out to snatch me against her burning bosom. I dropped the shovel and twisted away, out of her infernal grip, tiny red sparks glowing in my clothes where she had touched me. I dodged the master chief when he rushed me and I was wild through town, leaping sidewalks and swimming canals, crawling up the ascending ladder through the heavens, lightning and thunder biting and snapping at me until I sprang pinch-toed out on deck into the sunlight. My smoldering clothes took just one breath of fresh sea air and I burst with a WHUMP into a fiercely burning flame.

I had never seen a person on fire before, and if I had seen a person on fire, I think I would have watched it. When I came out from the engine room and burst into flames the crew did not seem to notice. Even the Idiot ignored me as he stomped something in a corner by the winches. I rolled in icy water pooled in a loop of leaking sea hose. I had been a small fire and in this way I was quickly doused. The crew stood around John in the stern beside the stinking corpse, waiting a turn with John's small telescope. There was something out past our diminishing wake that was following us, something that had the crew leaning over the stern rail, squinting and guessing and cursing, something more interesting than seeing somebody being on fire.

Bare-eyed, Lonny said he could make out a white hull and a blue light closing in on us fast, and John said their signal lantern read *Somebody did something to somebody*, he couldn't quite read it all yet, and the two men in prison blues stepped back to take counsel, eyeing the lifeboat, patting the knives and sharp shanks hidden in their clothing, a Told-you-so from one and a Not-now-I'm-thinking from the other. The weeping man said *Fuck* and sobbed into his shirtfront, and Ira Dench said *I told you I knew that rogue-waving boy was bad luck from the beginning*, and I knew that rogue-waving boy he meant was me, this boy, Fishboy, laying out of flame in a cold bath of salt water, thinking, *The white hull and the blue light are coming for me, for what this somebody did to somebody.* I lay there thinking, *The signal lantern flashes IF I JUST ACHE, BEER OR WINE*, spelling Fishboy, the somebody who did the something to somebody, Big Miss Magine.

I lay on the deck in the looped seawater pool, my eyes closed, listening to the men beg John for a turn with his small telescope. Near me the Idiot began grunting for a turn with the telescope too. As he stepped over me to go beg John, the Idiot's shadow darkened my eyelids. I looked up in time to see his slow-moving foot pass close over my face, his crimson heel thick with crushed beak and small brown feathers.

I had seen knothole seamen in my days as the Fishboy living in the cartonated encampment, men so long at sea that on first landfall they will break free the stiffness from their trousers and make themselves in knotholes of barrels and planks, in plug openings cut from fresh fruit. I have seen knothole seamen make themselves in slitted canvas bags of fresh shellcut, claiming it the best, the merchants later wagonloaded with it saying *Nothing revitalizes vigor better than produce from the sea.*

I was thinking of knothole seamen while I sat in the dark bottom of a barrel John had dropped me in to discover the criminal on board our ship, the somebody who had done something bad to somebody from the flashing lantern's signal. I was thinking of knothole seamen when I felt a warm thick fluid drip into my scorched tuft of hair, felt the fluid ooze down the back of my neck, thinking John's fluid would be so large that in it would swim tadpoles of children.

I sat in the bottom of the barrel not having thought

John would be a knothole seaman, but you never can tell.

The stuff began to crust in my hair even as it dripped down my neck and forehead, and when I wiped it away from where it stung my eyes, I looked at it on the back of my hand and saw that it was red, as if the anointment was Big Miss Magine's blood back again on my wrist. I was guessing John had found me out, had discovered what I had done, until I heard him tell everyone to reach inside the barrel and touch my head, that I had conjurer in me, that I would call out when the criminal touched me, innocent men had nothing to fear from me.

I was no conjurer, I was not like the feeble men who drifted through the fishhouse in the spring to summon up the dead all day long for a crust of bread or a nickel or a penny. I was not one of those feeble men who shook conch shells filled with pebbles and talked in twisted tongues, flipped on their backs in the sand, their eyes rolling and their heels kicking, the people standing around watching, waiting for a message from Bubba Samuel or Sister Sister, or from some fever-ridden infant who couldn't speak a word anyway before it left this place. I knew the ways of conjurers slipping around my cartonated box the first night looking for a tip-off, looking for a snitch about the next day's people's names and dead, and then leaving the last evening through my camp again, drinking all my soup when they said they wanted just a sip, drinking from my Hessian bowl, their hands cupped around its rim to calculate its empty weight. Across my fire I could see the veins in their eyes broken from skull-rolling, and in their bloodshot eyes I could see they would murder a thing as small as me for what little I had, and they would murder me without fear that when they conjured up the dead I would be among them. They knew their incantations conjured only the living foolish; the voices they claimed to hear in their heads were just their own stifled laughter.

I did have a sweet spot on my skull that when you scratched it hard enough it would be like the place on a dog's spine, the place where if you scratch hard enough the dog's leg will quiver and itch. I did have the sweet spot that when I scratched it hard enough my eyes rolled back a little and I clucked, but it was not to conjure up the dead, it was not to swindle the foolish. I was not a conjurer.

Reach in the barrel and touch the conjurer's head, John was telling the crew, saying an innocent man had nothing to fear. I saw the trick in getting the truth, I saw that John would hand over whoever the white ship with the blue light was coming for. I saw that John would let nothing hinder his net-pulling, would let no ship follow us for long to foul his precious snare, and I saw the trick in it as I had seen the trick before, when someone at home had stolen a piglet, and a wise woman put the found pig in a dark shed and said for all the suspects to reach in and stroke it, saying the pig would recognize the thief's touch and squeal, and all the suspects except one came out of the dark shed with hands black with soot the woman had secretly rolled the pig in, the sootless one having more faith in an old woman's sayings and a pig's intuition than the trustworthiness of his own guilt.

The first hand down inside the barrel was Lonny's. I could tell it was Lonny's by the way his fingers gently located my face and began to stroke my chin in a way that a man should not stroke a boy's face. He was careful not to touch my hair. His fingers moved along my jaw, caressing, and then I felt his thumb rudely plumb between my lips and I bit him, tasting tar and salt, his hand snatching out of the barrel.

The weeping man's hand came quivering toward my face next, the wet and snotted fingers of a blubberer that contracted into a fist as his one word crossed his mind. And as his word crossed his mind he squeezed his fist so tight that it dripped a tear before it withdrew, careful not to touch my hair.

There was bunched-up string in Ira Dench's fist when he lowered it into the barrel, and for a moment I wondered if it was a one-handed cat's cradle of fortune he would spread open between his fingers to let me read, to show me with moving twine and knots the rogue wave he was sure I was bringing to the ship, and when he opened his fist and let the bunched-up string fall into my lap I saw that it was patterned with knots, and I thought maybe Ira Dench was giving me a gift like the hemp bracelet he wore, a round Turk's head with long-eye braids, good-luck diamond tassels, and tiny monkey fists, but when I picked up the bracelet I saw that it was not a bracelet for my wrist, it was a hangman's noose for my neck, a fancy gallows knot small enough for a child, nine tiny wraps marking the lives of a cat, a looped lanyard end from which a quick lynching could be accomplished anywhere aboard the ship. He, too, was careful not to touch my hair.

The next hands came in tandem, tinkling of shackle. One hand opened and closed and flitted around my face, a fleshy butterfly that teased my eyes and tickled my nose, and I laughed as a child would laugh because I was just a boy, and when I laughed the other hand seized my throat and shut it, the butterfly now a cupped hand across my mouth stifling my choking sounds. I pulled at the hands, kicking around, and then clawed the rough sides of the barrel until I ripped out a jagged splinter that I drove into the flesh of the strangling hand. My crusting hair still remained untouched.

My crusting hair remained untouched until a large strong hand plowed into its roots seizing a firm purchase, and I was lifted out of the darkness holding my hangman's noose. I was lifted up into the dull silver halo of sun while the Idiot whistled and honked, showing he could reach in the barrel and find what the others could not find; braying and baring his teeth, he lifted me up to show me to the men all around, showing my red gooped hair, John's trick to the truth betrayed by a trumpeting ass.

John chewed his beard and looked at the paintless hands around him. Around him, the men looked at their paintless hands. Only the men in prison blues began to speak, and they both spoke at once, they both spoke of blame and tried to confess ahead of the other, to confess and then to beg John to save them, and John told them to be quiet, that he would save them the best he could, that he would hear their confessions later because the white-hulled ship was bearing down on us. John said he would save us all, and I think he said that because he saw that to turn over all the guilty men on his ship would be to turn over his crew, his net menders, his net handlers, the men he needed to pull his precious net aboard.

We'll try the pox ploy, said John. *We'll run up the pox flag and paint our faces with the stuff from Fishboy's head.*

The crew stood around me and laid their hands upon my head. They dabbed themselves with the crimson paint, each man applying it as he thought pox might corrupt his skin. The prison men, who had seen a bit of plague, sprinkled the paint around, the Idiot bathed his face, and Lonny seemed to prefer a single dot on his forehead.

The men touched and rubbed my skull to apply their diseases, and their rough fingers and sharp nails scratched at my sweet spot. I fought it at first but my eyes began to roll back a bit when my sweet spot was sweetened, and my vision rose. Beyond their arms, over their shoulders, and above their heads my eyes considered the whirligig sky. I could see the black ash clouds racing toward the sun, and as the men rubbed my skull harder I saw higher, the sun itself. In the conjured moment, the sun, like a drowning man, reached out one last time from the swirling pool of clouds and pointed to us all.

We were boarded by the white-hulled ship at noon. It slid alongside us, its crew bearing plastic rifles, its big blue light clicking on its mast. The white-hulled ship had not been put off by the pox flag we flew, crossed yellow bones on a field of red. John had hoisted the flag from a sea rover's hope chest for safe passage, colorful tokens of contagious diseases and slippery allegiances.

The white-hulled ship was not put off by the sheriff's corpse Lonny and Ira heaved over the stern into its path, the sheriff's bloated face painted the pox-mark red. The sheriff's boots filled with water so that he stood in our slow wake, rolling and bouncing behind us like a toy you cannot tip over.

The white-hulled ship was not put off by John waving it away with his muleskin cloak from where the ship was about to slice across the top of his net. John's hands trembled when he saw it happen.

Just before we were boarded John slung the two men in prison blues into a bosun's chair and hung them over the far end of our ship to make them harder to find. They sat side by side on a rope-held plank used to fix and paint the hulls of ships. Their feet dipped in the water, they gripped the ship's skin with homemade devil's claws they had constructed from ragged gloves and sharp spikes. They were frightened of John, the white-hulled ship, and the water all at once.

Lonny had wanted to hide in the tool shack and come out swinging his axes, severing heads and arms,

Like at that lady's birthday party? John had said, and Lonny said that time it had been machetes. John talked Lonny out of that plan, and then John talked Lonny out of his next plan, to wrap his ax heads in rags and pretend they were crutches before he attacked the white ship's crew. *But I do a good cripple,* Lonny said to John.

John told Lonny, Ira Dench, and the weeping man who said *Fuck* to lie around listless and sick-looking. John said he was not worried about the Idiot. With all the talk of hiding, the Idiot had found for itself the perfect ostrich arrangement, him sitting in full view on the main hatch with an empty nail keg stuck on his head.

What about me, John? I said to John, and John knelt beside me in a way I thought at first to comfort me. What he wanted was to reach in my hair and fix his pox makeup.

You stay close to me for the sympathy vote, said John. He said with my missing ear, my burned-up head, my weird eyes, and my puniness, I didn't even look human at all. John dabbed paint on the backs of his hands and blotched his cheeks. *How do I look?* said John standing and cinching his rough muleskin cloak and I said he looked fine.

The white-hulled ship slid alongside us, its crew dropping bumpers between the ships and grappling our rail with gaffs.

Request permission to come aboard, said their deck officer.

Oh no! said John, Pox! We all have the pox, and you'll catch it. We're dropping like flies.

Yes, said the deck officer, *we recovered a body you put over.*

Yeah, that was poor Bob, said Lonny, trying to make his voice weak. *That was Bob, the bobbing body. Bobby, we called him,* and Ira Dench's fraudulent moaning was broken by a laughing snort.

Our Medicine Man said he died of slashed throat and disembowelment, said the white ship's deck officer, and Lonny said it had started as a tickle in his throat and a stomach ache.

Do you have your documents? said the deck officer to John.

We are just humble fishermen dying of the pox, said John. *The crew is just these men, my father the captain, and my two sons you see here, an idiot and a freak.*

The deck officer looked at us all. *I want to speak with your captain,* he said, and he motioned a boarding party of men with dark glasses and plastic rifles past us.

Our captain is sick also and is probably asleep in the wheelhouse, said John.

The deck officer told his men to find our captain and when John lifted his fillet-sharpened hand to stop them plastic clicked around us and gun muzzles were put in our faces.

I'm sure you'll find the captain resting, said John, and I began to worry that they would drag Mr. Watt out of the wheelhouse into the burning sun.

The white-hulled ship's boarding party went forward; I could hear them banging on the wheelhouse hatches.

John asked if all this was really necessary. His painted pox was thinning with his sweat, the red places melting and dripping down his cheeks and neck.

The deck officer said he had been pulled off search and rescue to find the person or persons responsible for knifing a Negro and then fleeing aboard a ship that matched our description. *Do you know anything about a recent murder ashore?* said the white ship's deck officer.

Before John could answer, the boarding party said that the wheelhouse hatches were locked, that they were going to go in through the galley.

I was worried about Mr. Watt. I wondered if his muscles would come undone if someone tried to grab them.

I wondered if someone's confession might save him.

I wondered if my confession might save him.

It was me, I said.

Which one is this, the Idiot or the freak? said the deck officer, and John said I was mostly the freak.

The boarding party made their entrance into the wheelhouse by crawling through the dog hatch from the galley, and now they made their exit from the wheelhouse by shooting out the smoked glass and climbing through its frames. The boarding party came running, dropping their rifles and losing their hats in their haste to reboard their own ship.

Let's get out of here, said one of them, *Whatever they've got, we don't want to catch it.*

You should see the captain, one said, throwing his leg up onto the white-hulled ship. *It'll make you sick to see it. I've never seen a pox like it.*

I'm going to give you a break this time, said the deck officer, backing away. *I could hold you all in the brig until we see some documents. You and your faking crew and your idiot freak children. You'd round out the circus in the brig with the crazy cook.*

Cook? said Lonny, lifting his head from the deck.

He says he's a cook, between fits, said the deck officer. *We have him in a straitjacket now. Before we had to lock him up he baked some delicious breakfast pastries. Then he had these fits and beat his head bloody against the cabinets.*

What kind? said Lonny, getting to his feet.

Buzzing fits, said the deck officer, *like there is a buzzing in his head.*

No no, I mean what kind of pastries, said Lonny, and the officer said they were kind of a croissant with cheese-butter fillings.

The white-hulled ship's Medicine Man appeared and began spraying powder along their rail, spreading a white film over everything, dousing the boarding party from head to foot.

This so-called cook, where did you find him? said John.

We picked him up on search and rescue, said the white deck officer. *We picked him up just floating on his big belly out to sea. There's been eruptions and land-slides ashore, and the water has been full of stuff miles out.*

A cook! said Lonny.

It sounds like my long-lost brother, said John. *The one who's fat, cooks, and is crazy.*

The deck officer asked John if he would identify him and take custody and Lonny said *Absolutely.* A cook!

They would only let John and me aboard, and only with the Medicine Man spraying us with white powder as we stepped down narrow ladders into the brig. On the way down the Medicine Man told us how they had found the cook in the litter of a landslide and a flood, how a tongue of muddy water had been pulled over the horizon, swirling eddies rippling and tinkling. *A waterborne pastorale* is what the Medicine Man called it, and I tried to imagine the picture he painted for us, the white ship sailing along a muddy lane, the trees of the forest laid over and mainsailed by their crowns, ruddered by their roots, crewed by bark-hugging squirrels and shivering field mice, birds' nests emptied into the sea, the eggs plucked by fish jaws beneath *(Lots and lots of sharks around, o god yes, we haven't found hardly any bodies so far except this live one, and this one is a live one, believe me)*, insects settling in swarms in the branches, bees like marbles rolling in beehive trays broken loose like sacked desk drawers. The white ship sailed along the muddy sea lane and saw a water-logged flock of sheep just starting to bloat, their pens and stiles now latticed, now broken singularly into driftwood fencing, blades of grazing grass and rips of turf rolling in the water, dirtying the sea, and in it all, this man, a big belly ballooning like a man-o'-war jellyfish *(that's what we thought it was, the biggest maybe we had ever seen)*, hands like flippers, an angry face, the white ship coming down off the country lane and across the undulating ocean meadow to the rescue, and the man flipping his hands and feet like flippers and fins saying *Go away! Leave me alone,* the sun-rouged face, his big belly crowned red, some sort of rash or welts like fallout from a volcanic navel. *Go away!* backstroking, fending off the gaffs and boat hooks, even slinging a turd or two, half drowning, having a fit, finally grappled by the shoulders, the Medicine Man giving him a needle in the buttock, putting him asleep in the brig clasped in the straitjacket embrace.

You talk too much, said the deck officer to the Medicine Man. The deck officer unlocked the gate to the brig and led us in.

I was in the theater before I got drafted, said the Medicine Man to John.

Somebody must not have liked your skits, said John.

NO! NO! Please, no, I beg you! said the cook when the deck officer told him his brother was there to claim him. *Anybody but my brother!* said the cook, and he ran his head into the bars of the brig and then fell to the floor rolling in his strapped and buckled jacket.

Hello, my brother! said John, and the cook stopped his ranting and lifted his head to look us over.

You have your arms, you're not my brother, said the cook.

Of course I have arms, said John, *the better to embrace you.*

104

That is not my brother, the cook told the deck officer.

He's just a little silly from banging his head, said John. *You know, the head banging, the dim light, that's all it is.*

There's not much resemblance, said the deck officer.

That is NOT my brother, said the cook.

Well, look at me and then look at my son, John said to the deck officer and John pushed me forward.

I guess resemblance doesn't run in your family, said the deck officer. *Will you accept custody and sign for him?* and John said that he would.

I have no idea who these people are, said the cook.

We'll have to have that straitjacket back, said the deck officer. *He comes the way we found him, no clothes. Sign here*, he said.

The deck officer and the Medicine Man went into the cell and brought the cook out into the light.

Wait a minute! said John. In the light you could see that the cook's face and bald head were bumped with thick red welts.

This man has the pox! said John.

The white officer smiled. *Here is your receipt*, he said.

No, really, this man really has the pox! said John.

The Medicine Man released the cook from the

straitjacket. *Brother!* said the cook to John and John fled the brig with the fat naked cook chasing behind him.

Actually I don't know what he has, the Medicine Man said to me. *He says he has bee stings but I've never seen so many bee stings before, if that is what it is. Of course, I've really never seen pox before either. I was in the theater before I was drafted to be a Medicine Man. Sometimes I can set a broken bone and sometimes I can't.*

As the white-hulled ship with its clicking blue light cast off from us, John stood on deck and shook his fist up at the white officer. Behind him Lonny, Ira, and the weeping man who said *Fuck* were watching the cook flail around in a fit. *Watch out for your brother!* the white officer shouted to John. *Watch out for his fits!*

It's just bee stings! said the Medicine Man, and they laughed at us as the white-hulled ship heeled over and plowed the black water under a fresh plume of exhaust.

*A*s the wake of the white-hulled ship rocked us I ran forward to the wheelhouse, dodging the scuffling men on deck. Twice the rumored cook had made it to the rail to leap overboard and twice Lonny and Ira Dench pulled him back and put him in headlocks and half-nelsons. They held the cook so tightly that his eyes egged out, and then his head vibrated with the noises he heard in it. The cook flung Lonny and Ira Dench off, rolled off his big belly, and made for the rail.

Let him jump! said John. *He's got the pox.*

We're hungry! Lonny said as he tackled the cook again.

They said it was just bee stings, said Ira Dench, kicking the cook's legs out from under him.

Forward in the wheelhouse I found Mr. Watt on his side in a dark corner, the floor slick with his muscle mucus and blood. Mr. Watt had been knocked down by the boarding party and had fallen on the shards of black smoked glass broken out by their hasty exit. Propping up Mr. Watt, my hands left perfect seeping prints in his shirt where I touched him.

What was that all about? he said, and I said that the white-hulled ship had come for somebody, and when he said *Somebody who?* I told him they had come looking for somebody who had done something bad to somebody black.

Somebody who had done something bad to somebody black? That's rich, said Mr. Watt.

Who did they arrest? Did they arrest Lonny? said Mr. Watt and I shook my head no. *Did they arrest Ira Dench, or the* Fuck-*saying man, or John?* and I said that they hadn't arrested anybody, but they left us a cook who had the pox. Mr. Watt laughed so that my worry for him fell away a little and I started to pick up pieces of the broken glass and put them in my shirtfront.

We always get the cook we deserve, said Mr. Watt.

Mr. Watt had been burned by the sunlight that the boarding party had let in; the red meat of his muscles looking scalded. John came forward and said *God, Watt,* and turned the wheel a few spokes so that our ship faced away from the setting sun.

Go get the men we hung over the side, John said to me, and I left John to tend to Mr. Watt.

I went away wondering what Mr. Watt had thought was so funny. Didn't he think Big Miss Magine had been good enough for me to kill?

The knotted rope holding the men in prison blues hung useless over the side of our ship like a broken rosary. The plank and rigging they had been sitting on had been bitten off by something that had come swimming up from the deep. The two men had saved themselves, their devil's claws dug into the years of layers of paint and hull rust. There were long scratches down the side where the ship had pitched and the men had slipped, slipping farther down so that occasionally they could kick at the snout of the thing that was swimming patient laps beneath them.

Help! one of the men said. His voice was hoarse and without expectation.

I untied the broken rope and leaned over the rail. I dangled the bitten-off end around the men's heads and faces, but they still pressed themselves to the side of the ship and did not look up. I could see that if they lifted their faces from the side of the ship and leaned back to look up, they would fall from us into the water.

Hello! they said. *Somebody's up there,* said one of them, and *John!* said the other. *Help us,* they said. *You said you would save us! We'll confess!* they said.

I was not John, and I could not have pulled them up even if they did grab hold of the knotted rope I dangled around them. They held themselves to the skin of the ship with their claws and they could not let go.

Help! the men said.

The knotted rope I offered was useless to them. If they had grabbed it I would have let go of it. I wasn't strong enough. I wasn't going to let the dead weight of these men pull me over the rail. I offered them the knotted rope as a sort of hope until help would come, but

John was in the wheelhouse and the hungry men were still butting the cook with their heads and trying to knock him out with shovels.

Only the Idiot came over, jealous of my new rope toy.

A swell washed the men's feet and the devil's claws slipped with the sound of fingernails raking slate.

I bounced the false promise of rope against the men. I tried to make the Idiot understand that he had to hold it tightly if the men grabbed it.

All right, John, I'll tell it, said one of the men. *But then you got to save us like you said.*

This isn't the normal us, said the other man. *It's just something that happened.*

Shut up, said the first man, *I said I'd tell it.*

Then hurry up and tell it.

The house was unlocked, said the first man. *The door was wide open.*

We broke a window, said the other man.

We couldn't see, the room was dark.

Dark? The whole city burning outside?

I fell over a busted chair.

It was a turned-over table.

There'd been a struggle in the room.

That's true. There was a cut-off arm in the fireplace.

Nothing to do with us.

That's right, we never cut off no arms.

We was only hungry and scared.

And we was looking for the king.

Shut up about that.

I'll tell it right if you don't.

Shut up. I'll tell it.

They had an election every year.

I said I'd tell it. Every year the richest man got elected king.

He was supposed to spend all his money.

All at one time.

For a big feast.

Music and drinking.

All his stock butchered and cooked up.

Free love on his wife.

I didn't know that.

That's what I heard.

I guess it was a small country.

The feast would last a week.

And after the feast he'd be poor.

But he'd be king.

I never heard that about the wife.

It was supposed to be a great honor.

Except the new king didn't want to be king.

They was having a riot about it.

They was running all around.

Looking for the new king.

They was burning the place up.

We was in town, unexpected like.

We'd busted out.

Shut up I said.

Sorry.

Coming in, people on the road said the new king had fled.

Just took off.

First they said he'd took his silver.

Just a couple of pieces, it being a small country.

But closer in town people said the king had fled with a bag of gold.

Then people said rubies and emeralds.

People running around, looking for the king.

They was pissed off.

They wanted to have their festival.

It was the law.

They wanted to feast and dance.

I didn't go for their music, though.

And free love on the king's wife.

Are you sure on that? I never heard that.

The toll collector said it.

He said that? Before you—

Shut UP, I said.

We never saw the king's wife.

We saw the king though.

I said I'd tell it. We saw the king.

In the house we broke into.

The door was open.

We broke a window.

We thought all the natives would be out running wild in the streets.

He didn't look like a king.

Nothing kingly-looking about having a ruby caught in your throat.

His face was purple, I guess.

He was up in the bedroom.

It didn't seem like a king's house.

It's a poor country.

I don't think it was the king's house. I think he was just holed up there.

Trying to swallow his loot.

Trying to make his getaway.

He was holed up, all right.

There was a boat waiting for him at the end of the pier.

He was holed up, turning purple.

I gave him a bear hug.

Out pops the ruby.

Size of an egg.

Personally, I can tell you, it's bigger than an egg.

Shut up, I said. The king was grateful I saved his life.

Just to take it back.

Shut up, I said. The king wanted to tip me but he didn't have any money on him.

Not ON him. That king jingled when you gave him the bear hug.

I didn't hear it.

Sure you did. I saw your eyes.

I never heard it.

Not even running to the pier?

The king said he would reward us later.

We ran down to the docks.

We had the king between us, a shawl over his head.

That must have been his girlfriend's house.

He knew it in the dark, all right.

That must have been his girlfriend's arm in the fireplace. The natives must have done that.

Probably to get her to talk.

It was a woman's arm.

Those natives was pissed off, that's for sure.

Those natives was barbaric. You should have seen the things they threw at us.

The natives spotted us running down the pier.

Longest pier of my life.

It was a big mob of them, torches and hollering.

Throwing them big things they had.

The king kept falling down.

Big long sticks with opened razors lashed to the ends.

The king said there'd be a boat waiting for us at the end of the pier.

They were throwing them things like spears.

I didn't know whether to trust the king.

A couple of the spear things landed around my feet.

I saw the king take out his knife.

One stuck right in the plank ahead of me where I was to take a step.

The king pulled his knife out under the shawl.

I looked down where the spear almost stuck right in my foot. It had a big red feather tied to the handle with a chain of bubble-gum wrappers.

I was starting to think the king was going to double-cross us at the end of the pier.

It had ARCHIE carved in the handle.

We was almost to the end of the pier and still I didn't see a boat or a mast or nothing.

Somebody spent a lot of time on that spear.

That's when the king fell on his own knife.

Do what?

It was dark at the end of the pier and the king fell, and he fell on his own knife.

You heard the king jingle and jank, and you slit open his belly for him.

He fell on his knife.

Then up pops the head of the sheriff, he's got the official town boat idling underneath the pier.

The king fell on his knife.

See, they was in it together, the king and the sheriff.

It was dark, the wharf was wet, he fell on his knife.

Up pops the head of the sheriff just in time to see you slice open the king's belly like you think it is a bank bag of silver, you slicing and holding out your hands to catch the money like a slot machine spun three cherries.

The king stepped on a corner of the shawl and tripped.

Only thing you got was handfuls of guts. Boy, was you surprised.

It was real dark.

I could see your eyes by the light of the burnt-up town and the torches here come the natives was bringing.

The pier was full of rotten places.

You promised the sheriff the ruby to help us escape.

Big knotholes in the pier, places where the tide had pushed the planks up.

Except I was smart. You say you the brains, except I was smart and swallowed the ruby myself.

The pier was slick with dew.

Good old me, just swallow any damn thing.

King's always got people around to keep an edge on his knife blade for him.

Guess I'm lucky you and the sheriff didn't gut me right there like you done the king.

Kings get nice knives, gifts mostly.

Man that'll gut a king in front of God, sheriff, and the general population throwing spears will just about gut anybody, I'd say, even a good old friend.

That knife the king fell on must've been like a stiletto, no finger guard on it.

You like to gut and cut, gut and cut.

Nice mahogany handle on that blade.

That's you, Old Gut and Cut.

Maybe it was laurel.

Next day you and the sheriff waiting for me to shit that stone. That sheriff was on to you by then.

What are you talking about? I don't cut no sheriff.

And I don't shit for nobody, understand?

Wasn't me who cut the sheriff.

You scared that sheriff, after what he seen you done to the king. That sheriff was smart, put us in shackles so you don't cut and gut me.

Sheriff was going to turn us in and get that stone.

You scared the sheriff and you scared the Idiot driving the mule wagon getaway. You a scary person.

I am not!

Yes you a scary person. Scaring that poor dumb Idiot, breaking his rabbit.

He was in with the sheriff! Waiting with the mule wagon getaway! The sheriff was going to turn us in!

You didn't have to break his rabbit.

I didn't break his rabbit. I thought it was for our supper. I was hungry, you was hungry.

I won't hungry with a big ruby stuck in my gut.

Just a idiot with a rabbit.

I bet it was his pet. You a scary person all right.

I am not!

Yes you is, you even scare me, you king-killing rabbit breaker.

Shut up.

Yeah, go ahead and hit me, see where it takes you.

At that, the king killer lifted his devil's claws from the skin of our ship to strike the ruby eater, and the ruby eater made a grab at the knotted rope to save himself. The Idiot gripped his end of the knotted rope and braced himself against the rail. I held the Idiot's shirttail between my thumb and finger.

Pull, John, pull! said the ruby eater, and the Idiot drew up two lengths of knotted rope. *I can't hold much longer,* said the ruby eater, looking up, searching for a face to plead into, the king killer looking down, searching for a dark-form mouth to keep out of, the flesh-wringing shackles dripping blood between them.

I could not make out what the Idiot was trying to say when he let go of the knotted rope. It was a strangled speech more painful and fearful than the noise he had made when he choked on the fishbone in the galley.

I let go of the Idiot's shirttail and leaned over the rail. We watched the foamy bubbles bloom in the water where the men had been delivered into the sea and I wondered how I would explain it.

Mr. Watt said it was bad luck to throw a piece of rope overboard when I told him what had happened. He said it was bad luck to throw rope overboard, bad luck to turn hatch covers over, bad luck to play cards while a net is out. He said there were always good reasons for superstitions, that rope can foul a propeller, that rogue waves could flood uncovered hatches, that a man with a strong poker hand will forget his nets and let them split with an abundance of fish. Mr. Watt said there was always a good reason for superstition, and I shouldn't have thrown the knotted rope overboard.

But I didn't throw the rope over, I said to him. I was

smearing warm lard on the places the sun had burned his inside-out organs and flesh. I tried to tell him how the Idiot let go of the rope while we were trying to save the two men.

Yes, but you untied it in the first place, said Mr. Watt, and I could not deny that. I had not denied it, even when John had asked me out on deck if I had or not, and I nodded yes. It would have been hard to deny anyway with Ira Dench saying he saw me do it, he saw me do it while he and Lonny and the man who said *Fuck* were fighting the cook. Ira Dench said he saw me look over the rail at the poor men and then he saw me untie their knotted rope.

You are an evil little boy, John had said to me.

I told you he was evil, Ira Dench said, Ira Dench, John, Lonny, and the weeping *Fuck* man having subdued the rumored cook. It was John who finally laid the cook out with one punch, one punch squarely in the face, the force of it laying the cook neatly on his back, a great weight dropped from a small height. We stood around the cook and watched his rubbery face decompress the pit the punch had made. An amber liquid oozed from one nostril, then more amber liquid slid from the other.

I think you ruptured his brain bag, said Ira Dench, and John said he hadn't thought he had hit him that hard.

Damn it, and I'm about to starve, Lonny said. *Nice going, John,* he said.

As we looked down at the cook and Lonny's stomach rumbled, there was movement in the cook's nose. It was not twitching like he was about to sneeze. The movement came from underneath the skin, like a mole tunneling through cropped grass.

The thing that crawled out of the cook's nose threading through his nostril hairs fell dazed on the cook's upper lip and swam on its back. It then lifted its wings and buzzed away. Another bee crawled from the other nostril, then two more, the makings of a small swarm, the last blown out by a snort, the last a large queen, trailing honey and a thread of snot.

Behold, the new cook, John said. *Try to keep your ax out of this one, Lonny.*

Lonny looked down at the cook and said *That's nothing,* and Lonny told his story of how a tiny sliver of steel had flecked into his thumb once when he was younger. Lonny said he had squeezed and squeezed the little hole the steel had gone into but it wouldn't come up. Lonny said his thumb swoll up to the size of a blackjack and was so sensitive it hurt for the wind to blow on it, and while I pretended to listen to Lonny's story I watched John go to where the bosun's chair had been tied and look over the rail. Lonny said one day he was up on a roof hammering shingles with a big hangover, a headache so big his thumb throbbed harder, his thumb so swoll the thumbnail was buried deep in the swelling with the skin cracked around it. Lonny said he was dizzy with the pain, the sun was hot, and he was thinking of just climbing down off the roof and getting a saw and cutting that fucking thumb right off, it hurt so bad.

I listened to Lonny and watched John's face darken, and I saw Ira Dench watch John stalking the deck and then look at me, and I knew I could not explain what had happened to the two men in prison blues.

Lonny said he could, when he was younger, drive in a nail with one blow of the hammer, and he was just going to nail in a couple more shingles before coming down off the roof to cut off his thumb with a saw when instead of bringing the hammer down in one terrific blow to the nail head, he brought the terrific blow down on his aching thumb, smashing it flat.

I saw John fill a bucket with cold seawater to rouse the cook, and I knew that he was rousing the cook because we were shorthanded to haul in the net, and I knew we were shorthanded because the two men shackled together had been lost over the side, and I saw that Ira Dench was anxious for Lonny to finish his story so Ira could tell John I had done it, Fishboy had untied the bosun's knotted rope, Fishboy, the little bad-luck rogue wave devil, me not even knowing they would be calling me evil too.

Lonny said he was no nancy, but in the pain of smashing his thumb flat he fainted right away. *But the best part,* Lonny said, *was when I woke up, I saw that all the infection had smashed out and in the stream of pus that had squirted across the roof I found the little silver sliver!*

Ira Dench was fast to congratulate Lonny on his thumb story and was quick to agree that compared to what had come out of the cook's nose, Lonny's story had beat him out, saying, pointing down to where the cook was doused in cold seawater, *Yeah, that's nothing, but John, where are those guys in the bosun's chair?* Ira Dench knowing I had untied their knotted rope, them not even in the bosun's chair, them just hanging on to the paint by their devil's claws. I knew I would not be able to explain that to John and Ira, I knew I could not explain how a large shark had come along and the Idiot had let go of the rope, so when John asked me if I had untied it, all I could do was nod yes.

I did not think that what I had done was evil or was bad luck, I told Mr. Watt, and Mr. Watt said that there was a reason for everything, even for the white ship to leave us with such a strange cook, the cook who sat in the cold water of John's dousing, his head suddenly cleared of the noises within, the taste of honey on his lips. He said there was a reason the white-hulled ship had come looking for somebody who had done something bad to somebody black, and a reason it had gone away without arresting John or Lonny or Ira or the man who said *Fuck*. Mr. Watt said it could have taken any of them but it had not. Mr. Watt said Lonny last month slipped away from where he was supposed to have been filling the water tanks with a slow hose, slipped away to a bar, a black man in there stacking dimes on the edge of his glass on a bet. Lonny being in a hurry, the stack of dimes fell into the glass just as Lonny ordered a drink. The man grabbed Lonny's collar and Lonny apologized and offered to buy the man a drink, offered to pick up any dimes that may have fallen on the floor, and Lonny bent down, and just as gently as a fancy tailor fitting some pants to get a good inseam measure Lonny slipped his knife into the man's ankle and brought it up all the way to his crotch, the man's leg open perfectly along the inseam through trouser and muscle so that in his first step the man's skeleton stick of bone walked right out of his leg. That was just last month, Mr. Watt said. Mr. Watt said they could have come for Lonny but they had not, they had not even come for the weeping man who said *Fuck*, who Mr. Watt said used to be so happy in love that his singing while he mended John's nets drove everybody crazy until they were blown ashore one night and he found out he was husband number six on his number-one wife. *That was an awful fix we barely got him out of,* said Mr. Watt. Mr. Watt said after the weeping man had killed his wife with one of her husbands he sewed them together the way he had first found them, thousands of stitches, the bodies black with stitches and then black with flies as the stitching together took days. When he was through stitching them together he began to cry at what he had done and was only able to speak his one word. His neighbors found him slithering along the road-side trying to crawl beneath rocks, trying to fold mudbanks over himself for an early burial. The man broke from his neighbors and they found him weeping and saying his word at the bottom of a muddy well, and when they took him home they found his handiwork, his signature in his stitchery. It made the papers, Mr. Watt said.

I lathered Mr. Watt's sun-scorched neck with the lard. He said the white-hulled ship could have come and taken anyone it wanted, John with his jugular jabbing fingernails, Ira Dench who doubles his fortune-telling string as a garrote. *Somebody doing something bad to somebody black. That's rich,* said Mr. Watt.

The sun was setting early behind a high wall of pumice smoke and steam and I lit a candle to see better where to apply the lard. I held the candle up to Mr. Watt's face forgetting his sensitive albino-like eyes, but it did not seem to matter, his eyeballs remained fixed, the pupils large and open. I began to touch the lard in places around Mr. Watt's face and he flinched as if he had not seen the approach of my greasy fingers.

Let me tell you about somebody doing something bad to somebody black, said Mr. Watt. *Once, when I was about your age,* said Mr. Watt, *I had to leave my country. Everyone was starving. I had to run at night and sleep in logs during the day because of the way I looked and because of the sun. I wandered into a rocky region where the soil was poor. I came across a small stone house, a house like I would like to have one day. The house had a small door and no windows, the yard was strewn with the chewed heels of shoes. There was a small well house and I was so thirsty I didn't hear a large dog come up behind me. I felt his breath on me, his hungry mouth watering at the way I must have smelled like raw steak to him. The dog growled and an old black man with coarse red hair came out of the stone house saying Who is there? I answered that I only wanted a sip of water and then I would be on my way. The old black farmer cocked his head and said it sounded like I was hungry, too, would I like some soup?*

I had not eaten in several days, and with the dog following and growling, I entered his dark stone house. I thought at first there were no candles because he had eaten them, and then as he searched for an extra bowl, I could tell by the way he reached around his shelves, I could tell the man was blind.

The blind farmer told me his wife had died early in the famine. They had not eaten the planting seed like everyone else had because the farmer said that would have been giving up hope. There was only chaff bread and water, and the farmer could not see that the wife was giving him hers to eat, and so she starved. The blind farmer had survived the winter eating his dead wife's shoes, throwing the heels to the dog. In my hunger I drank the soup, and it was rank with leather.

I accepted the farmer's invitation to spend a day and a night to rest. The dog's mouth foamed when it was around me so I stretched a hammock made from an old sheet in the rafters above the well. I was unaccustomed to sleeping at night, so I joined the farmer in his rocky fields, turning over the soil, hauling stones, planting wheat by moonlight, the sun not mattering to the blind farmer, him finding it easier to work in the coolness of the evening. I stayed for several weeks, working at night, sleeping in the well-house rafters during the heat of the

*day, the old blind man napping in his windowless house.
We lived on rough chaff bread and his dead wife's shoes,
throwing the heels to the dog.*

*The wheat sprouted and my hair grew even longer,
covering my shoulders and chest. The large dog was
weak and friendly, so sometimes I would go into the
blind man's house after our work was done. I would sit
and listen to him talk about his wife. One day when I was
brushing my hair with my mother's brush the farmer
asked me to brush my hair outside. He said the sound of
it was too painful, it reminded him of his wife brushing
her hair, so I went outside and sat by the well. Later the
farmer came to the door and asked me to come back and
brush my hair inside, so I did. I brushed my hair in the
darkness, listening to the old man cry.*

*After bringing in the small crop we were very ex-
cited to bake the first loaf of bread. While the farmer
ground the wheat and made flour I washed my hair in a
bucket by the well. I let it dry down my back. My muscles were wrung out from swinging the scythe and my
hair cooled and soothed me.*

*That evening, as we sat and waited for the bread to
finish baking, the large dog growled at the door. I was so
accustomed to living with the blind farmer that when I
went to the door I forgot what I looked like to the world.
In the yard, a crowd of people had gathered, and when*

they lifted their lanterns to my face, they screamed and fled, calling for pitchforks and torches and pikes. Living with the farmer had helped me forget I was on the run from what I had done to my family. I thought that the people were part of a search party hunting me down. I thought my guilt was larger than the smell of fresh bread baking in a hungry, famined land.

I told my friend that I had to leave. He said to wait until I at least tasted the fresh baking bread. I told him he would be in trouble if he was found giving me refuge. The farmer did not understand. He stroked my hair and said goodbye. I let the dog lick my hand and I was out the door.

I had just made it to the well house when the mob returned and shouted for the devil to come out of the house.

Make a light and show yourself, devil! *the people shouted. The old man said there was no light and the old dog barked.*

The crowd said Hear his blasphemy and hear him barking! The demon! Luring innocent hungry people to their death with the smell of baking bread. See how the yard is littered with the shoes of the dead! See how his fields are empty at day and tended at night by spirits! Come out, devil! *they said.*

Come in, *said the blind farmer. The bread is done*

and out of the oven. There is plenty for all, come in and eat.

We won't be fooled! *said the mob and they tossed torches at his door and threw a cover over his chimney so that the old man was driven out into the yard by the choking smoke.*

The people threw their pitchforks and their pikes. I hid in the rafters of the well house.

When the blind man and the dog lay dead in the yard the people brought out the loaf of fresh bread.

Don't eat that, that's the devil's bread, *some said.*

The people looked at the bread.

Maybe devil bread won't hurt you, *someone said.*

They looked at the bread.

Maybe he really wasn't a devil, and we can eat the bread, *somebody said.*

As they ate the bread, they poked at the blind man's body.

Probably not a devil, but strange-looking eyes, *they said.*

Yes, *they said,* surely not a devil but surely looking a lot like a devil. Anybody can see his eyes look like a devil's eyes might look like. He shouldn't have been looking like a devil and baking bread, *they agreed. When they finished eating, they collected their tools from out of the farmer and his dog and they all went home.*

I wasn't sure what to say after Mr. Watt finished his story. Was I supposed to beat his story like Lonny beat the cook's? Was I supposed to beat his story of somebody doing something bad to somebody black with my own story? I didn't want to tell him that somehow his story had made me hungry. I finished covering him in his burned places with the lard and on purpose passed the candle close to his face. I saw where the sunlight the white-hulled sailors let in had burned him, and now I saw that the sun had also left him blind. I didn't know if he knew that yet, and I wasn't going to tell him, especially after his story. All I could think of to say was to thank him quietly on my way out the wheelhouse door.

Thank you for the rich story, I said in my lisping whisper.

I seemed to be getting along with being useless pretty well but being evil was something I was going to have to make friends with. I was useless to John when he tried to haul in his net that night, useless to Lonny running the winches, useless to the other men, who tried to take the meshes aboard. The crew could not get more than a corner of John's precious net aboard, and John was worried that they would tear it. Black Master Chief Harold came and went, cursing and cursed by John who asked for still more power. I was only helpful in stirring John's anger when he saw me, the evil boy who had drowned the two prison men, and I was sure John thought he was only two men short of bringing the hundred-ton net aboard.

Useless was pretty easy to work into. I sat on the outside wheelhouse steps and watched the turning stars while the men struggled with John's net. Useless was easy, evil would be something else. I wondered how far back the evil started in me, figuring an absolute place to begin would be sticking Big Miss Magine with my butter-turned knife. I could see how evil was working its way right along with me on the ship, from smacking the Idiot upside his head with the big spoon to having no intention of holding on to the knotted rope if the prison men had tried to grab it. I watched some stars fall and wondered if soon I would begin walking in a crouch like a housebreaker beneath a window. I wondered if I would begin holding a hand inside my shirt like I was holding something I had stolen, or like I was concealing a dagger. I wondered if I would begin to take up spitting.

I had just been thinking how much more work being evil would be than being useless when the aft deck went quiet. John worked the men until both winches broke and the men's hands were raw and bleeding from trying to haul in the sharp-wired cables and slick ropes by hand. The men fell around exhausted on the deck and John packed a bundle of net-mending tools and twine to repair the places in his net the white-hulled ship had sliced with its propeller. I stayed hidden from him until he dove over the rail, swimming deep. Giving evil a try, I damned his soul, cursed his return, and spit.

A small lantern burned on a cord swinging random shadows around the winches. Lonny went to sleep on the main hatch after turning out the decklights. He tried to get the Idiot to sleep alongside him, for warmth, he said, but the Idiot preferred to sleep in a lifeboat. Left to themselves and tired, the men sought their own comforts; the weeping man who said *Fuck* covered himself in rotting finish fish and mud from where a bottom net had lain, and Ira Dench, in preparation for the rogue wave he was certain I would be responsible for, finally went topside to lash himself to the mast.

When I saw Big Miss Magine come walking out the aft cabin door and sort through the pile of finish fish I had thoughts I would never have believed I could have thought. My first thought was to hug myself with homesickness, wondering if ever I would be back safe and warm, smelling damp cardboard where I drooled and dreamed asleep in my cartonated box. Then I thought how glad I was that Big Miss Magine was not dead after all, that maybe she would forgive me and I would let her go ahead and snatch me up and blow that blue breath of hers on me. Then I thought *Wait a minute, this black bitch may have been trying to kill me to eat me, and here I am playing nice when I should be playing evil,* and the evil thoughts were the ones I was going to work up, and while Big Miss Magine picked around the finish pile of rotting fish and groceries I went to where Lonny's big axes were crisscrossed on the hatch. I took hold of the handle of one and started to drag the ax quietly across the deck. I betted that old bitch had never seen so many finish fish to choose from, and I was going to send her straight back to hell with an armful, and as I drug the ax up closer behind her, I had another funny thought, and that was that for a dead person she didn't seem to float very well, her footing in the slimy fish was slippery, and then I figured that was just the rigor mortis set in, making her arms and legs stiff and achy, and I felt bad for a second thinking I had caused that, until I got myself worked up again to heave the big ax in one arc, one arc all I had strength for, to cleave Big Miss Magine in half like Lonny would a cook.

I knew, being evil, I had hate in my heart but at the last moment I could not find it, and that was just as well, because the ax was too heavy to lift and I dropped it on the deck.

Big Miss Magine turned slowly around with her armload of finish fish. Her swirling blue fog breath wreathed her face. I backed away, bracing for whatever she was about to do to me, and I saw she had a hand-rolled cigarette hung in the corner of her mouth that spiraled out blue smoke, and in the dim brown light I saw her face was bristly with old beard and spotted with poxlike welts.

What the hell is with you? said the rumored cook, and I saw that it was just him, an armload of old fish and groceries, Big Miss Magine's stolen dress the only thing he could scavenge to fit him from the things the crew had robbed from the cratered lake people, the neckline torn and already sweat-soaked from his lighting a fire in the galley stove.

I was just going to help you, I said, and I made myself useful collecting fish and showing him where the lanterns were in the galley to light the place with.

All night I scraped the galley table, chipped out the oven, swabbed the floor, and scoured the sink. In the dimness of the lantern light I watched the rumored cook, I watched him bent over the fish he filleted, the globe shade cutting off his head, Big Miss Magine's dress split-

ting at the seams, his legs like her legs, the same coarse
dirty brown feet, his calves spotted with red marks that I
leaned to see if they were pox welts or bee stings, not
being able to decide either. I worked and watched the
cook, and I could tell he wanted to ask me a question, but
for hours he did not speak to me.

I wondered if it was up to me to warn the rumored
cook about the possibility of being severed into two
pieces. I wondered if Lonny would kill him. I wondered
if Lonny would split him in two with his ax. I wondered
if this was the type of cook Lonny hated, the kind I heard
about when the union-scripted ships were in, the cooks
with the loud complaints against the crew that they
feared while at sea, cooks brave now on land to admit
that maybe the pork and potatoes they had served had
been spoiled a little from leaving them out too long in the
weather beneath the companionway steps, or from not
icing the groceries properly in the hold or forgetting to
ice them at all. *To hell with you heathens! Just give me
my fair share!* these cooks would demand, each tucking
his full share into his apron pocket along with the money
he had made selling the rotten grocery remnants to the
black women going home on the purple bus. These cooks
with idle hours and bunks forward above the oven,
bunks that they did not have to share in rotation, bunks
warm and dry when the watches would come in with ice

in their beards and bleeding hands for a cup of coffee the cook had let grow tepid because he had been reading a detective novel and had fallen asleep with it spine-split on his snoring chest, the crumbs and buttery brown flecks of hidden-away private desserts littering his coverlet. Cooks that always seemed to have friends in every port with a carriage or a car to take them into town to cash their checks in the last five minutes of the last banking day at the week's end, waving and honking as they drove past the bone-weary and burned-out sailors hitchhiking into town to miss the bank's last bell, to miss having pocket money for their forty-eight hours of liberty before another forty-eight days at sea. Cooks who taped pinups along the galley walls of beautiful women with their legs spread and their breasts just so, the cook's running commentary punctuated by a pointed ladle — *See the swell curve here, the ankles on that one!* —waving the ladle above the seated sailors, dripping on their heads the thin gruel their hungry stomachs grumbled for, a soup thin and gristled, the cook having cut away the lean meat for his own pot pie simmering with peas and carrots in the back of the oven. Cooks with a coat of clean finery folded away in a dry locker, away from where the other sailors had to stow their garments in canvas sacks, clothes that never dried, clothes tossed from bunks and flung from hooks to the floor in the ship's pitchings and rollings, clothes stepped on by comatose sailors going on watch and trampled by staggering men seeking sleep, clothes smeared with winch grease and mud from the ocean floor, wet, fungoid, and torn, never the time to mend a tear in them like the cook had time, like the cook had time at midnight, his detective novel put aside, some herbal tea before retiring to his warm bed over the oven, the cook primly stitching a button onto a greatcoat stolen from a friend's closet in the last port of call. Cooks, the first to leave ship with no deck watch and the last to report aboard, just as the ship throws off its lines, just as it is about to ease itself from the dock, the cook strolls aboard, all the time in the world, deposited dockside by a carload of painted women, the worst hag better than any of the other sailors has known, the other sailors having had to sit aboard and play cards and throw knives during their forty-eight hours of liberty, their paychecks read and folded, read and folded all weekend in their pockets, folded and uncashed, missing the bank's last bell by fifteen minutes after the cook had driven past, some generous soul trading a thousand-hour-carved scrimshaw to some lowlife dockmaster for a small bottle of cheap rum for the whole crew, a whole weekend, some scrimshaw sweetheart across the sea cheated of her treasure. A cook, strolling aboard reeking of cheap perfume and flushed with brandy, his stolen overcoat pockets full of candies and tins of store-bought tobacco, strolling aboard in a real shirt and real trousers, never ever a cook dressed like the rumored cook I was looking at, a poxy naked cook covered in a sheer homespun cotton blue-and-green-flowered dress more drape or dropcloth than dress, the thing our rumored cook stood in at the sink while I watched him skinning a fish with no complaint, a nagging question in his head instead of buzzing bees, and watching him in the dim lantern light I thought maybe he was not the kind of man I would have to warn of Lonny's double-headed cook-splitting axes after all.

Draw me some flour, the man said to me.

I took up the sifter and opened the dry locker I had been sitting on studying the cook. There was a bag of rice, a block of salt, and a stale sack of flour that the large black rat was guarding.

Don't touch me, don't fuck with me, I'll bite your little fucking arm off, so help me I will, said the rat and I let the top of the locker drop.

What's the matter? said the cook, and I tried to tell him there was a rat in the locker.

A rat? I can't abide rats, said the cook, and he picked up a wooden meat mallet but when he opened the locker the rat was gone.

Don't run tricks on me, said the cook, and he said it without anger in a way that I knew he wanted to carry on talking, and I was right about him wanting to ask a question, I was just wrong in the way I didn't answer fast enough.

The cook asked me his question after he scooped a sifter of flour and was taking it to the counter to make dough, and I could tell it would be an important question to him that he was trying to ask in a way that made it seem like a small question to ask a small boy.

Are there any men with rubber arms aboard this ship? he asked me. I did not know if I had heard him right, and then I had to make a list of everybody so far I had seen and try to remember if they had real arms or rubber arms. The cook took my few seconds to answer as an answer, yes, that there was somebody on the ship who wore rubber arms, and he dropped his sifter of flour and shook me by my own arms. *Tell me which one it is,* he said, and this new side of the cook made me worry that there might come a time when he might be split in two if he carried on like this with Lonny, and that made me worry that I would have to be the cook again. I did not want to be the cook again. I wanted to leave this world in whole pieces.

Any evil I had erased from myself pitching in in the galley working and thinking good thoughts about the new cook came back to me when I lied and pointed to the bolted hatch that led to the engine. *Down there,* I tried to tell him.

Instead of being afraid, the cook seemed relieved and let go of me. He seemed relieved at least to know where a man with rubber arms might come from to get him. *That's good,* said the cook. *That's real good. I'll be waiting for him.*

I didn't tell the cook there wasn't any rubber in this world that wouldn't melt in the infernal engine room. I didn't tell him a rubber arm couldn't crank the latches on that heat-swollen hatch. *Stupid cook,* I thought at the man when he went back to making his dough. If my mouth hadn't been so dry from the fright he gave me I would have spit on the floor.

The cook went back to filling large pots with water and setting them on the stove to boil. He went to the engine room door and tried it, and came around me so that I could see he was thinking of one last thing to say to me, something that would put me in his confidence to help him wait for the rubber-armed man. It was late into the night, and I had known men who were strangers to each other gather at my cartonated encampment just to sit by my cypress-knot and fish-wrapper fire to get in out of the dark and burden each other with things on their mind, things they would never tell anyone in daylight, things that made them, in the morning, shake off each other like they shook off the frost that had grown on them in the dark before the dawn, avoiding each other, taking separate paths out of the fishhouse lot even when the night before in the camaraderie of the road they had promised to travel together against scavenging animals and maybe even against men like themselves.

The lantern light was low and the galley was lit mainly from the blue flame flowering beneath the pots. The cook sat across the table from me, and I knew he was going to tell me a story about a man with rubber arms, whether it was a true story or not. That did not matter. It only mattered that he wanted to tell it, and was going to tell, and I would listen whether I wanted to or not.

My brother Brune and I are from the north country, said the cook. *We have been sailors all our lives. Brune spent several years seal hunting. He was first a boat puller, then he was a shooter. I saw him once after a typhoon, our wreckage had washed together in the sea.* Help me, *my brother said. My brother's arms had been broken by a falling spar. He feared the men on his wreckage would eat him next, that is how things had become. We are starving here also, I told my brother. We had lost all our officers and I was only acting captain because I had saved the sextant and was the only one* who knew how to use it to shoot the sun and the north star. The men aboard my wreckage pushed my brother and his cannibals away from us with gaffs and sticks of timber and soon the sea that separated us curved to the sky. I waved to my brother but I did not cry. I had not seen him in sixteen years. He could not raise his broken arms, either to wave to me or to curse me. His eyes were hollow, his mouth hung open, and I felt I could hear his last breaths.

We had a seer aboard our wreckage. At the time of my brother's sighting, the seer said I am afraid you will see your brother again.

The cook paused in his story and rolled a cigarette. Above the hum of our engine I could hear the two-whistle snore of the Idiot outside on the hatch.

The cook lifted the globe from the lantern to light his cigarette. When he leaned into the flame I saw that the pox marks on his face had deepened into scarlet.

In the north country, where Brune and I are from, said the cook, every spring when the snows melt, the water fills a basin that warms over a hot place in the earth. The earth begins to steam and the mud is rich and black. The elders believe the mud has great healing properties. Families dig trenches for their elders and bury them up to their faces with shovels, then they scoop out places for themselves. It is very soothing. The elders *feel revitalized and the young men feel potent, the young women feel fertile. Do you understand me so far?* said the cook and I nodded that I did. I did.

Every year in the stand of firs near the basin we have Black Night. The aldermen of the village make a lodge by bending sapling firs and lashing their crowns together. The floor of the lodge is made soft with fresh sprigs and ferns. In the middle of the lodge a fire is kept low, kept low and made smoky by adding green branches.

One night every year when the black basin has filled with mud and the elders feel revitalized and the young people feel fertile, the married couples of our village take the mudbath together and then enter the lodge. The light is smoky, the floor is soft and sweet, and everyone swims together in the living mud.

Do you understand? said the cook and I could only think it must be like when certain fish spin and wriggle in the mud of low tide during a spawning moon. I nodded yes.

All winter, said the cook, drawing on his cigarette, *all winter when it is bitter cold, the men of our village wait for Black Night. During the three-hour Sunday services in our church, the men study the necks and wrists of the women sitting around them, anything that would tell them who they will be in the dark, and after service, leaving church, the men are courtly and bow, shaking the hands of other men's wives to calculate their weight. There are meanings in everyone's eyes.*

The confusion in my eyes must have betrayed me because the cook said impatiently *Look, Brune looks like the butcher, I resemble the portrait of the mayor hanging in town hall. Our sister looks like her mother. Our village is strong and vital.*

On the afternoon our wreckage parted, said the cook, *I was certain I would never see my brother again. I was not raised in our church to believe in seers. The seer's fingers dipped the water while he slept one morning and a large fish pulled him from our raft.*

With the sextant, I was able to sail our breaking-apart raft into a port that had been leveled by the typhoon. The fishing fleet had vanished, the docks were just a few poles leaning in the mud. The only ship at anchor was a slaver just arrived from the wilds. The slaver had lost its first mate overboard in the fringes of the storm. My crew cursed me for delivering them into such a sorry place. I packed away my sextant and signed aboard the slaver. I had little choice, said the cook.

The cook said that setting sail, he was surprised to see so many black crew members, that there must have been some sort of mutiny. He said that as he set them to work mending the rigging and working the gear, he was able to tell a difference between the black men who were the sailors and the black men who were cargo below. He said he looked for the difference in their speech and in their look, but where he found it most was in the way they smelled.

Is the smell because of their shipboard diet? the cook said he asked the captain, and the captain said no, that everyone ate the same basic rations, the same wormy biscuits made into wormy mush by adding rancid water, the same rotting rations of salted horsemeat, although the sailors were allowed more of it. The captain told the cook the difference in smell was where they came from. The captain said the sailors were from the coasts and rivers, crafty water traders, and the human cargo was from the landlocked interiors, from tribes trusting and communal. *If you notice,* the captain said to the cook one night after their dinner, *the sailors still smell of fish and rainwater, while the slaves still smell of game and fruit.*

The captain drank some more wine and offered to show the cook what he meant. The captain opened the door to his large closet and chained inside was a beautiful black woman. *A king's daughter,* said the captain. The captain said he already had a buyer for her in the next port, a black gentleman who had made a fortune selling his brothers.

There were two, twins, the captain said to the cook,

but the other refused to eat and died. *I had to put her over the side at night through my own porthole. It can't be known there is a woman on board, especially a beautiful princess. Smell her aroma, the cook said the captain ordered him. I believe she has eaten nothing but rose petals her entire life.*

I did not smell rose petals, said the cook. *She smelled of human terror and of fir trees. It is more like a forest smell,* the cook told the captain, and the captain said that was only his closet, lined with cedar. The cook said that after the captain had revealed his secret to him, he became suspicious of the cook and took away his sextant.

Once, said the cook, *late on a dogwatch, I was relieving myself over the rail and turned just as the captain was coming up quickly behind me. The captain tucked his arms back into the folds of his greatcoat. It was clear that he had intended to push me over, but I had smelled his approach. We were entering the northern latitudes and the nights were getting cold, and he had taken his greatcoat out of his large closet. In the instant of my last dribble over the rail I had first gleaned homesickness then lust from the waft of cedar, then the smell of terror that turned me around; the scent of the woman on his greatcoat saved my life.*

The cook paused in his story again as men do when

they are recounting how close a life was to becoming lost, and he paused the proper length of time owed to him in his storytelling since the life nearly lost had been his own.

The cook rolled another cigarette and continued his story.

We met great floes of ice entering the northern latitudes and posted two lookouts in the bowsprits with lanterns at night, our sails reefed. We were able to sail slowly into a port that was within several days' journey of my home village. I intended to visit my parents after we had unloaded our miserable cargo and had been paid.

I did not recognize the old port I had shipped out of as a boy. There were tall buildings in the city, and there were warehouses and landings on the opposite shore of the river where once there had been just forest. A harbor clerk was rowed out to us and we were taxed. It took two days for a slip to become open for us. When I was finally ashore, the streets smelled of exhaust and manure and hot grease.

My captain was less suspicious of me when we were being paid although he gave me a short share. The black princess had already been put ashore in a trunk. After I was paid I tried to go back aboard to reclaim my sextant but a sentry from the shipping company with a musket held me off at the gangway.

My earnings would have lasted little longer than a week in the city, so I planned to return home as soon as I could. I took a cheap room near the wharves to rest before beginning my walk home the next day. The cheapest sleeping pit I could find was in the back of a warehouse near the slave quarter. I was sick ashore, still pitching with the roll of the ocean. I think I had a fever. I could not erase the image of the black princess from my mind. There was no heat in the sleeping pit, and I found myself wandering the slave quarter. I went into an auction house where it was warm just as the bidding began.

I bought a seat in the cheapest section of the house, in the third tier where sailors and peasants and pimps sat, men hoping to buy a field hand or a whore or an apprentice from the affordable sick and diseased lots of slaves paraded through the platforms below us. It was in the third tier that I saw an old mate of mine bidding on a cabin boy for his captain. It was in the third tier that I saw my brother Brune.

I leaned back on the bench before he could see me. I wanted to look at him, the butcher's son from my mother. My brother, his armless shirtsleeves pinned to his breast so like wings that in my feverish thoughts I expected talons at his feet. His face was red from years at sea and his scalp was sun-spotted yellow. His scurvy mouth was empty of teeth, and he was howling, keeping the other bidders a width away on the bench. I saw that he was being watched from the aisle by a large purser's bailiff.

When my brother caught me looking at him he raged at me. Brother! Brother! You bastard! *he said until a large part of the third tier looked at me so that I had to go over to my brother to quiet him.* Look what you did to me! *he said, spitting froth.* You left me, and now look!

I could not deny what he said. His mates aboard the wreckage had refused to set his broken arms and they had become gangrenous, and had been amputated by the surgeon on the frigate that had rescued them from the water.

You owe me! *shouted my brother into my face.*

Yes, yes, quiet, *I told him. The bidding on the auction floor was continuing.*

I recognized a face or two in the first lot to be auctioned off, the lot being the remnants of a mutinous crew that had been in prison so long that the lamplight was too much for their eyes, their skin was broken and yellow, and their legs were rat-bitten. An officer from the admiralty court stepped up and presented the auctioneer with a writ. The men were taken away to be formally reconscripted into the navy and then hung.

The second lot were gangs of the black captives we

had brought and the bidding from the pit was busy. Often, agents from trading companies bought entire lots of men to send across another ocean. After the lots of gangs were sold, the pit emptied except for men smoking small cigars and traders making out their checks and adding figures on ledgers they balanced on their knees.

Now the auctioneers brought out the women who would be sold as domestics and whores and wives, and the men below us in the second tier shouted and the auctioneer pounded the table with his gavel. My brother began to scream and froth at the mouth again. He was so loud that I struck him and immediately felt bad for having struck an armless man until some men seated on the benches in front of us turned around and encouraged me to strike him again.

As the men in the second tier stood to bid I began to recognize some of them as being from my village, and I realized that some of the young men I had known years before had become elders themselves. I wanted to call out to them but I was afraid I would be thought to be making a bid, so I kept my seat.

I felt ill again. My head burned with fever and the room pitched. I rested my head on my knees. I saw that my sea boots had split at the heels, the first time they had been dry in over a year. I looked over at my brother's clumsily shod shoes. They were neatly laced and tied, and I wondered who had tied them. I looked to his shirt-sleeves and wondered who had pinned them to his breast. My brother was beginning to shout again. The auctioneers had finished with a group of indentured servants who had run off, and were bringing out another lot of women.

When they brought out the Negress princess the men around me were on their feet at the sight of her. The sight of her even near death made me want to speak words I could not think of. My brother began to rant, but this time only one head from the second tier turned to look at my brother, and I saw that it was our father, our mother's husband. After sixteen years, my father's look to me had only one meaning, and that was to strike my brother if he became a bother.

My former captain, the slaver, stood in the wings and shook his head at the low bids being offered for the princess. Had the black gentleman trader refused delivery because of her apparent illness? The stiffness of her new modern dress seemed to be all that was holding her up. Her beautiful tar skin looked dusted with pumice, and the bidding fell off further when the rumor swept the tiers that she was dying. The captain's face in the wings was set on a resignation of loss.

Suddenly my father was standing before me demanding my wages. I gave him a few coins. I felt fever-

ish. My father opened my brother's pockets and took his paper money. I must have the Negress, my father said. He stood in front of me. Your mother is dead, he said. Give me your money.

The auction house rolled and pitched and then I felt as if the whole building had stem-struck an iceberg and reeled shuddering from the impact.

The cook paused to pick his nose. On the fingertip he held close to the lantern I could see what looked like a wing from an insect.

The next thing I remember, resumed the cook, *I was riding in the back of my father's cart laid alongside the unconscious Negress. For several miles out of the city I saw that the land had been cut over and was empty except for washouts and stumps. A few tall firs stood around a stone cottage here and there but the great woods I remembered as a boy had been cut down and hauled away.* Ship's timbers, for the war, *was my father's only explanation on the long road home, my armless brother sitting beside my father on the seat of the cart, turning around to grin and stare at me and my father's new bride.*

The first stand of young firs I saw were the ones being bent into a lodge by the elders of my home village. My home village was in ruins, sacked and burned during the war. The elders that were left were digging with all their strength into the hard black mud. It seemed early for Black Night. The ground was still mostly frozen, only a little steam was escaping. Good, good, said the men when they saw my father's cart draw into the path. They came up to us and helped my father pull his bride off the cart. They played with her fingers and rubbed her hair. They helped my father home and left me to finish digging their trenches in the cool mud. The war had taken the young people from our village and the elders were impatient to be revitalized.

My brother and I could not take part in Black Night because we had no wives. The elders of the village came down by torchlight to take their mudbaths before entering the fir tree lodge. Our father brought the princess, his bride. She was wrapped in a dark red curtain I remembered used to hang in the front parlor of my mother's house. The black princess's fingers were curled at her throat and her eyes were closed as our father rolled her to the mud pit on a handcart.

In the light of the torches I helped the elders of my village lay in their trenches. I filled in the mud over their bodies with the shovel and smoothed the breathing spaces around their faces. Their bodies were very old. I could not bear to look at some of them.

After I was done, I was sick with fever and exhaustion. I felt the earth shift beneath my feet. I crawled into the lodge with the smoky fire and the soft sweet floor and fell asleep.

I woke up before dawn. I could hear scraping and digging in the mud, and the first thing I thought of was wolves. There were no more wolves. They had been killed and their dens broken open by timber cutters and soldiers.

The mist was light, and in the light I could see my brother. He was kicking the mud away from our father's new wife.

I must have her, my brother said. *Help me. He could not stand in the coarse mud on one foot and dig with the other. I could see he had already lost a shoe in the mire.*

Help me! my brother said to me. *You owe me!* he said.

Stop him! said my father, waking from his sleep. *My father's face opened like a white flower I had seen bloom once on the black slope of a volcanic island. On the island it had just rained for the first time after an eruption, and white flowers with pretty red centers bloomed before my eyes.*

Stop him! said my father.

Help me! said my brother.

My father's shouts were waking the other elders from the village, but they did not feel revitalized. They had lain in the pit too soon in the season and they could not lift themselves up from the cool mud that had hardened in the night.

Help me, stop him, help me, stop him.

I remembered standing on the slope of that volcanic island, in just a few wisps of escaping steam, and I remembered watching the white blooms with the red faces the rain had opened. The rain had left sweet sheets of clouds like morning mists that rose up to the rim of the smoking volcano. I felt the heat of the earth through my boots, I felt the earth shift itself over a hot spot sprung up from its core. I watched the white petals of the beautiful flowers bloom and then fade quickly to brown in the heat, their pods of seeds bursting and spilling down the mountainside and into the cracks of the rocks. I smelled nectar and I smelled sulphur. I heard the mountain rumble. I heard my father call my name.

I opened my eyes and saw my brother crush the white bloom of our father's face into the mud. I watched my brother stepstone the white blooming faces of our elders, each time letting his weight ease the face deep into the mire. There's a little nibble from the mailman! said my brother and he drew out a bloody heel. He stepped his way around our blooming faces until the mountainside was quiet, its flowers wilted brown, the flowers' seed scattered.

Where is she? *my brother demanded of me, slop-ping around in his muddy work.* Where is the Negress? *he said.*

My brother had churned the black mire with his barefoot and one-shoe'd trompings so that it would have been impossible to find where the Negress was buried, the way her face blended in the mud.

Help me! *my brother pleaded.* You owe me! *he said, and I finally said* All right, here is your help, *and I threw the shovel into the mud beside him. And that is how I wanted to leave my brother, my brother pleading and crying as I began to walk the road back to the port city. I would have left him like that, crying and yet alive, when just as I climbed from the edge of the pit I heard the Negress cough, and my brother heard her cough, and by her cough he found her and began digging the dirt and mud away from her with his foot and clumsy shoe in a way that made me think of a hungry animal scratching at a buried scent of something dead.*

I don't know if it was that the Negress was young or that we had buried her deeper in the mud than the rest, but sometime during the night her fever had broken, and as we uncovered her nakedness, her eyes opened and were bright and searching, and it was clear that she feared my brother and me as we lifted her from the earth.

Do me, do me! *said my brother and I knew what he*

meant, he meant it in the way he wanted me to unbuckle his pants like my father unbuckled his pants for him to piss when my brother said Do me! on our journey home. All right, I'll do you, I said to my brother, and I swung the shovel so that when it struck my brother's head I felt the force of the blow resonate through the handle I held, as if I had struck a great dull chime.

It took several blows to my brother's head until he lay still in the mud. The last of the blows were not so musical. They rang hollow and flat.

The hole I dug in the black mud to bury my brother was so deep that at its very bottom hot water began to seep into it like the ocean will seep into holes dug along the seashore. The hole I dug for my brother was steaming when I pushed his body in and shoveled the mud. This was not how I wanted to leave my brother, but it is how I left him, I left him and took the black princess away with me in my father's wagon.

We stopped at a roadhouse and the Negress ate everything the innkeeper's wife put in a bowl before her. Her eyes were less frightened-looking and the way they shone at me I imagined things I would say to her if I could speak her language. She did not like for me to be out of her sight for even a moment, and seemed intent to sleep with me, and that night in her native way she was amorous, and I began to realize that spending the night in the black mud had revitalized her, that being buried in the mud had brought her back from death, and as I fell asleep in the Negress's arms I had a dream in which I realized my grave mistake.

The dream was so vivid I roused the innkeeper and paid our bill and bought a fresh horse for the wagon. Before light we were moving again, the dream so sharp that with every image of it that I remembered, I whipped the horse harder.

In my dream I walked back to my home village, back to the young fir lodge and the Black Night place in the ground. The heat in the earth had pushed the elders' brown wilted faces to the surface of the mire here and there and that did not surprise me and it did not frighten me. What frightened me, the part of the dream that has kept me moving through my life, was how true and real the next thing I saw was, and the next thing I saw was the open eruption in the middle of the mud, the place where I had buried my brother, a place freshly kicked open from within, the fresh prints of a revitalized bare foot and a clumsily shod shoe leading to the road from which we had escaped.

The lantern on the galley table began to sputter staccato light on me and the cook and the cook turned the wick down so that the only illumination was the dull boiling flames beneath the fish stew pot. I had lied to the cook when I said there was a rubber-armed man down in the engine room but now that my words were out in the world it almost made it seem real that maybe someone armless was hiding beyond the engine room door. I was frightened by the story the cook was telling and I was tired, too, tired in the way that what he was saying set dream pictures going off in my head, especially since the galley was almost completely darkened.

The princess and I fled the country, said the cook. *For a long time I could not explain to her what we were fleeing from. I could not explain how sometimes there is certainty in dreams. We never actually saw my brother but I could feel when he was close. For several years we avoided port cities where I was certain my brother would seek us.*

We would settle into a place, my princess taking in laundry and me learning to cook, and then I would hear about a man with wooden arms, or plaster arms, or ceramic arms with metal snippers and pincers for fingers. My common-law princess wife and I would flee to another place, a place especially away from seafaring cities and from cities roamed by veterans of wars in which men's limbs were shorn with swords and cannonfire.

We finally found a hotel where my wife became the concierge and I became the cook, and we had the last of our five children. I had a photograph of them all that I lost in the landslide. I had been unbothered by my brother for years until I began to realize that I had forgotten what my brother looked like. I had only spent those two days with him as an adult, and his face as I left him, as I remember him, had been disfigured by the shovel.

One evening a patron at the hotel said that at the last place he stayed he had seen a man with rubber arms. The patron said the man with the rubber arms had been ranting in the streets, saying it was time to confess our sins against our brother. The patron said the man with rubber arms was saying Ye must be born again as I have been born again. I knew in my heart it must have been my brother the man had seen.

I loaded my children and my wife with what we could carry into a wagon and left our town. Barely had we made several turns on the valley road when the earth shook and we slid into the sea. I lost everyone, I lost everything. I awoke in the ocean tangled in the crown of a floating tree that was thick with bees. You know the rest, said the cook.

I was not sure if I did know the rest. I had been told stories before by people around my cartonated fire that were meant to frighten me and disturb my sleep, and the way the cook told this one, and the way it was already working on my dreams, I thought maybe the cook was honest and cruel, but I was not sure. I thought that if what he told me was a lie, then he knew I was lying when I said there was a man with rubber arms in the engine room. I figured I would just have to wait and watch the cook watch the engine room door.

I lay my head down on my folded arms. I dozed off and woke up when the cook snored. I raised my head to look out the porthole and saw the first chalky smear of the sun rising. It was not comfortable sleeping at the galley table. My neck was stiff and my left arm was pins and needles, so that when I sat up my arm hung against me like a dead weight. I tried to twist some feeling back into it when suddenly the cook started up from his sleep. He was on me in a heartbeat with the rusty meat cleaver.

Who is this? he asked and I tried to shout *Fishboy Fishboy, my arm's asleep,* but he said *Make a fist with that rubber arm or by god Brune I'll hack you here and now.* I still had the pins and needles so I was slow to raise it. The blood flowed back into my arm and I managed to make a fist I shook in his face.

Just be glad, said the cook, and he sat back down in the corner.

I made sure he saw that even though my arms were puny they were more real than rubber. He saw it all right, but I felt his eyes on me until the morning star rose and tangled in our rigging.

A loose timber from the sun's sunken wreckage floated up and was dawn on the water. In its cool red light you could see how the waters around us were disturbed from beneath. Globes of old air rose to the surface and shattered, spritzing blooms of kicked-up mud. Mobs of waves rushed crowded swells, slapping faces and knocking caps off to the wind. Lonny watched the confusion as he stood at the stern pissing patterns across our wake.

I think John's got him one, Lonny said as he tucked himself into his pants.

About twenty lengths behind us the ocean parted and a giant shark danced on its tail with John hunkered on its back. John's backside bounced just forward of the dorsal and he rode the shark with one hand high in the air and the other sunk deep in a gill.

He's a fucking bucking bronco, Lonny said.

John drove his charger alongside the starboard rail, close enough so we could admire the denticled topskin of the beast, close enough so we could hear John's ribs creak to keep his lungs from bursting, close enough so we were doused in spray as the shark thrashed to dismount its rider. The two disappeared deeply again.

Lonny gathered his axes and put a pelican hook on a large lifting line. *Somebody told John that a shark ate his girlfriend*, Lonny said to me. *Get you a hammer or a lead pipe to bash its head in when we bring it aboard. It's a big one*, Lonny said. *John hates sharks*, said Lonny.

There was nobody else out on deck to help us except the Idiot. The weeping man who said *Fuck* was still somewhere covered in the garbage pile along the rail and Ira Dench was lashed tight to the mast above us. The cook was in the galley where I had left him earlier. I had slipped away when I thought he was trying to teach me how to cook.

You don't want to scald a soup to death, the cook had said to me and I said no. He said *You don't want to gut big fish without bleeding their tail*, and I said no. *You don't want to wring off the head of a crustacean until just before he's dead*, said the cook and I said no, and I kept saying no until I could slip away out on deck where Lonny was pissing over the rail.

John surfaced sidestroking, dragging the shark backwards by the tail to drown it.

Hey! he shouted.

Lonny tossed the hook end of the lifting line overboard to John and we had the shark by the tail. Lonny wrapped the line around the winch head and set the gears to work. The weight of the shark pitched our deck as the creature inched up over the side, half drowned, still twisting and snapping. Lonny took in more line as John climbed aboard and I stood back from the beast which was half the length of our ship.

He'll try to fight us on the deck, Lonny said and just as soon as the shark touched down and there were a few pounds of slack in the line the shark came alive ripping and smashing the top hatches into splinters, snatching and snapping into pieces the planks and tools Lonny and John had used to ease the beast aboard. The deck was slick with water and slime and we all, even John, slipped and fell trying to run away forward.

John said *Here's a bullfighting trick* and he came down from on high with a long spike through the shark's snout. Coughing up blood-speckled foam, John put another line through the shark's gills and pulled the lines tight around the winches. The shark lifted suspended off the deck.

The cook appeared in the aft cabin door, a pot of coffee in one hand, a clutch of mugs in the other.

John pushed his sharpened fingernails into the shark's throat until the white skin tore. Handful by handful he tore at the shark's underskin. The shark chewed the air it swam in, seeking the source of the blood it smelled. John tore farther the white underbelly and things began to fall to the deck: a sheep and a wagon wheel, boulder-sized boluses of squid and fish, a pumpkin. John tried a backhand fillet with his fingernails, raking long rips in the skin, and there was a bloody rain of flying fish and an oil drum boomed down. There was the stench of digestion. Working his knifelike fingers over a large knot near the anus of the shark, John gave the carcass a good tearing pull.

Out of the carcass fell the forms of the two men in prison blues, their uniforms dissolved and their skins burned white from the acid in the shark's stomach. Their eyes were closed and we thought them dead at first, goopy blood of hemorrhage from their noses, their eardrums split with pressure, their hair gelled to their heads like newborns'. The slithering stench of sea death that they lay in inched them toward us and we all held our breath, and one of them turned his head toward us, and I was sure that it must have been the ruby eater because when his eyes opened there was nothing but shattered red within to see by.

The cook stepped forward and put two mugs into shackled hands. *You boys look like you could use some coffee,* he said, and he poured them some.

John rummaged through the shark's offal and I wondered just what clues he was looking for, a girl's hairclip or a girl's bonnet, or a girl's thighbone or skull.

Lonny stretched the skin of the shark carcass and roped it open above us. The way Lonny made a shelter of the shark reminded me of the way the long summer boats rigged canopies of canvas against the sun. The men in the boats used to give me odd twists of driftwood that had snagged their nets, driftwood they would carve a bit into two-headed snakes and crocodiles. I was daydreaming about ever playing with those wood scraps again when Lonny came along and pressed a shovel into my hands.

We followed John and shoveled over the side the things from the shark he had already looked through, the rotted eyes and livers, the lungs and guts of creatures the shark had eaten. We shoveled the debris the shark had snuffled up from the bottom, mostly things thrown from ships, oil cans and bottles and plastic, and then we hit another stretch of the shark's mealtimes, some skinless organs, some float sacs, bladders, clutches of arteries, all undigested. Lonny found a bright red swizzle stick, he said, from a fancy ocean liner. He stuck the swizzle stick mast in a coconut hull and gave it to me as a boat. *We're best of friends now, aren't we, my little evil Fishboy,* he said, and I put the coconut boat aside until my work had been done.

John finished looking through the shark's innards and sat in the stern with his legs over the side. He spit out the seawater as it drained from his nose. He spit out the bloody speckled foam as he coughed it up from his chest.

He'll never find her, Lonny whispered to me. *Never in a million years,* he said.

The cook came out with a long knife and a platter to cut shark steaks. Lonny and I had just about finished shoveling the shark offal overboard. Between helping the cook, which carried the risk of learning to cook and being split in two, and helping Lonny, which carried the risk of just not being caught alone with, I chose helping Lonny. Lonny and I had just about put the mess over when the cook said to wait a minute. The cook lifted a bloody strap of leather from Lonny's shovel.

This looks like my old bridle, he said.

The cook sorted around in the pocket of what was one of the shark's mealtimes.

This looks like the face of a clock I used to have.

This looks like the handle of my wagon's wheel brake, and Lonny said *There sits a wagon wheel.*

The cook was desperate on the deck, wanting to know where the rest of the stuff was, and Lonny and I pointed to the large hole in the rail we had been shoveling everything through.

It could be anybody's stuff, said Lonny and he began to finish shoveling, and I wondered if what the white-hulled ship's Medicine Man had said was true about the landslides ashore, was this anything that could have been the cook's?

The cook said *You are probably right,* and he said it in a way like if the stuff was his and shark-eaten, it would be too much for him to know.

But as the cook reached down to gather his platter and rusty butcher knife, he picked up what had looked like a bloody purse. Inside the purse was an old worn book.

This is my poetry, said the cook.

The cook opened the book. I could make out big white pages of small black words wasting space.

Poetry, said Lonny. *I thought you was a cook,* and Lonny might as well have added *goddamnit* in the way he spoke to the cook.

The cook opened the last page of the book and showed us a photograph. In the photograph was a tall black woman and five light brown children.

This is my family, said the cook, and I had to look away from the picture of the Negress and the children. I looked down on the deck to see if any of his family might be with us. I saw that Lonny and the cook had the same idea but nobody said anything, just Lonny let the cook look through the remnants of the shark as John had done before, and then we shoveled the whole matter over the side.

*A*t sunset the cook came out on deck and rattled a spoon in a pot. *Dinner is served,* he said.

I had been sailing my coconut boat back and forth across the lifeboat Lonny had filled with seawater, Lonny figuring that that was the best way to keep the two men who used to wear prison blues preserved for a while, even though he did not give them through the night to live. You could look down into the lifeboat like it was a fishtank and see the two men bubbling at the bottom, a flounder resting on one's chest and an occasional lobster kicking around the other one's head. I tapped my coconut boat around in the water until I thought I could see one of the men let his arm float up in annoyance to snatch at it from below. I would lift my boat and the image of the men in the water would ripple apart. Once the Idiot tried to take my toy away from me and Lonny clubbed him and gave the boat back. *We're best pals, aren't we,* Lonny said to me.

Lonny had been trying to comfort John when the

cook said dinner was served. *There's some hope*, Lonny kept saying to John until the cook rattled the spoon in the pot. Lonny realized he had scrambled to his feet too quickly and had to stand beside John a little longer than he would have liked to make up for it. *We'll find her, there's hope*, Lonny was still saying, walking backwards.

No one had seen the weeping man who said *Fuck* since he had buried himself beneath the mud of rotting garbage. *All right, my friend*, Lonny said to the garbage. Lonny said he was as sentimental as the next person about whoring wives but enough was enough. Lonny turned the sea hose on the mound, breaking the stinking debris and mud apart. Muddy garbage ran in a river out the drain. Lonny laid the torrent of water top to bottom, removing first the rotten fish, then the black vegetables, and then the sour fruit. Soon all that was left was the sandy mound of bottom mud which Lonny flooded with the hose.

Lonny took the hose off the spot. Where the man who said *Fuck* had laid in the garbage and muddy sand for three days was just a scoured-bright place on the deck. There was no one there. We went to the rail and watched as the last of the washing water dripped through the drain. There was a curtain of sand crystals floating downward through the water. The tiny bits caught the setting sun in a drapery of sparkling remorse.

And to think he owed me five dollars, Lonny said. *Let's eat, I'm hungry,* he said.

For dinner that night we had grilled shark steaks, oysters on the half-shell with a chopped bean leaf and pepper garnish. Barracuda soup, tuber fruit sliced and fried, seaweed salad, boiled lobster, gourd casserole, thick biscuits, and mule-brain sweetbread cracked from the skull of our ship's figurehead. To drink the cook had wine, a gallon of methyl alcohol mixed with crushed hackberries.

Have some, Fishboy, Lonny said and he poured a little wine into a saucer for me. Maybe if someone else had been there Lonny would not have offered me wine. Maybe if John had not been sulking on deck, maybe if the weeping man had not disappeared or if Mr. Watt ever came out of the wheelhouse or if Ira Dench had not lashed himself to the mast, Lonny would not have offered me the wine and I would not have drunk it, but I did drink a little of it. It was worse than sucking a lemon but I liked the way it made me feel. When once while we were eating we heard Ira Dench holler *Rogue wave!* weakly from the mast, Lonny yelled out the porthole *Shut up!* and I stood on the galley table and stuck my head out the porthole and yelled *Shut up!* too. *Have some more wine, Fishboy,* Lonny said and I did.

We three ate, me and Lonny and the Idiot, and the

cook took up the plates as we finished them. The cook gave me bad looks. *Take some soup around to the others,* the cook said to me. He gave me a bucket of soup and a ladle, and a stack of bowls I put on my head like a helmet.

Go away, Fishboy, John told me when I went to him with the soup.

The water in the lifeboat where the shackled men lay preserving was dark and star-sprinkled. I poured some soup in the water and stirred it with the ladle.

Climbing the mast I spilled most of Ira Dench's soup.

Could you just pour a bit into my mouth? he said. His voice was hoarse from crying out *Rogue wave.* I held a little to his lips. There was barely a mouthful and it spilled out. He said he must have tightened himself too tightly to the mast. Behind him his stomach saddle-bagged his spine. I said I would loosen the ropes and he said *NO! Don't!* He said that would be just when the rogue wave would strike, when he was least prepared. He said just to tighten him up a little and be on my way. I ran my hands around him and found a place where there was some slack and pulled it out, and he thanked me in a stifled voice you could barely hear.

Climbing down the mast I put a step down on a rung before I was ready. I did it just as I was passing the empty bowl from one hand to the other. And maybe it was because the ship rolled, and maybe it was because I had been drinking a saucer of wine and had forgotten the rule of being aloft: one hand for the ship and one hand for yourself. And maybe the rungs were slick with Ira Dench's spilled soup and maybe even Ira managed a rope trick, tied up as he was. All I know for sure is that the bowl went backward skyward and I fell forward downward. I tripped on an antenna and spun off a high-wire brace. My fingers for an instant gripped a rain gutter until the rest of my body fell by and snatched me off. I pretty much struck the deck outside the galley face first and it felt like a bowl of salty soup had broken in my mouth.

I remember the cook holding me over the sink as things fell out of my mouth, some teeth, a bit of tongue, a torrent of food soaked in homemade hackberry wine. Between bouts of mouth-washing the cook went over to serve the galley table. Black Master Chief Harold and his boiler devil and fire lackey had smelled food in the vents, and later I wished I had been able to see how the cook acted when the engine room door had blown open, the cook expecting rubber-armed men and getting the charcoaled trio instead. They sat me down beside the black master chief when I seemed better, and I remember he smelled like chimney draft in a rainstorm.

Dazed and maybe even a little drunk as I was, I remember feeling the cook's popularity spread among the full-stomached men seated at the galley table. They watched the cook clean up the stove, they watched him put the platters and plates into soapy buckets for me to scrub later. His popularity soared when they watched him open his locker atop the oven overhang. They craned their necks to see what the cook had brought in his little leather satchel to hoard for himself, to save himself through the unexpected hungers and scurvy, and everyone saw that the locker was empty except for the little poetry book. There was no potted meat, no sweets, no medicine or mouthwash bottles filled with scotch, not even tobacco, the cook having to pick off the deck the men's butts to roll his own in tissue. The cook took down the poetry book and when he turned, the men were digging around in their pockets.

Black Master Chief Harold gave the cook a pouch of tobacco, his lackeys gave him matches dipped in wax and rolling papers. The Idiot gave him the rotting toe fetish on the string, and Lonny, teary-eyed with wine and love, stood up unsteadily and drew a fine bladder dagger out of his shirt.

Hey, cook, you want this? said Lonny, and I think we all wondered if Lonny meant *Where do you want this?* But Lonny handed the blade to the cook handle first and claimed he had personally stolen it from a church where it had been used to fillet the hearts from virgins.

Thank you, said the cook. And then the cook in a swirl of Big Miss Magine dress hem spun around and flicked beyond belief in speed the bladder dagger into a tiny target of pine knot in the door of the plate cabinet.

It throws well, said the cook. *Thanks, thanks a lot*, he said, and then he hawked.

He hawked again, something caught rumbling in his chest.

What! said Lonny.

Hawk! hawked the cook.

Oh god, said Lonny, Lonny retreating from the sound of rattling phlegm, embarrassed by the gift-giving that had tainted the after-eating.

The cook hawked again, leaning shouldered over the sink, shaking his head, smacking his lips.

I can't stand that noise! said Lonny.

Hawk! said the cook.

Spit, then, damn it! said Lonny. Lonny unhooked an unlit lantern and said he was going out to look at John's charts before he split something.

The black master chief and his lackeys went below after picking leftovers out of the pot of the next day's soup. Out on deck went the Idiot to break apart my coconut boat.

I lay back drunk and dazed in the corner of the galley. I lay back with no gift to give. The cook rolled a cigarette and lit it. He started coughing again, his face red with the effort to bring up what was hung in his chest. He coughed and hawked until he seized the thing up in his throat and sucked it into his mouth. When he spit it out, the thing spun through the air and landed squarely in the pot of the next day's soup. The cook balled up the rotten toe fetish and threw that in the soup, too. He sat down at the galley table with his poetry book and smoked his cigarette.

Stir the soup, he said to me.

I climbed up on the stove and stirred the soup with the spoon the size of a boat paddle. I was hoping that stirring soup didn't count as learning how to cook.

Stir it up, don't let it burn, said the cook, and he snapped the pages of his book as he read them.

I *am blind,* said Mr. Watt.

I know, I said.

Too much sun, he said.

I put a sharkfish sandwich into his hands.

What is happening? Mr. Watt asked me, and I told him Lonny was holding a lantern along John's spine as John lay asleep.

He's trying to read the charts, Mr. Watt said. Mr. Watt asked me if Lonny had been drinking and I said yes. *He'll probably end up burning John with the lantern and there will be all kinds of trouble then. Lead me out on deck*, said Mr. Watt and I put my head under his outstretched hand.

On deck Lonny was carefully blowing crusted sea mud away from John's tattooed skin revealing patterned islands beneath. When Lonny saw us, he said *Good, Watt, you read this chart. I'm lost already.*

I'm blind, said Mr. Watt. *Isn't that rich?*

No, it ain't rich, said Lonny. *How can you get blind when only you can read John's charts?*

I know them by heart anyway, said Mr. Watt. *Where did we leave off looking the last time?* and Lonny said halfway up the right side of John's shoulder blade.

That's a good chart he had tattooed professionally, Mr. Watt said.

These on his back are the best, Lonny said. *Some of the ones he did himself on his front are awful.*

John rolled his nakedness on his back and snored a

snore that tornadoed the ragged twists of his beard around his mouth. Lonny was quick to move from the sweep of John's arm, John swimming away from something in his sleep. The island chain Lonny had been studying broke leagues apart in a continental drift of skin and armpit.

Damn it, said Lonny. *Do you think we ought to roll him over?* and Mr. Watt said to let him be, that he could recite from memory the whole chart if he sat down and started at the beginning.

Lonny went inside to get his wine and left me holding the lantern by John's living cartography, the snoring of which fluttered the wind around my face and smelled of low tide. Mr. Watt sat on the hatch in the dark. He said not to get too close to John with the hot lantern, and to stay out of Lonny's reach when he has been drinking. *I'm finding blindness to be very pleasant, so far,* said Mr. Watt.

Mr. Watt said the story of John's charts began in the crook of his left thumb and forefinger, and I leaned in with the lantern and found the place. *That was the harbor John shipped out from, then there is a tempest around the wrist. In the tempest his ship's cargo of whiskey and malt shifted, the liquor spilling from broken plugs.*

And he drank some of it! said Lonny, Lonny taking

179

another swig from the methyl hackberry wine. Lonny did not offer me any wine and I was sure it was because Mr. Watt was watching out for me even though Mr. Watt was blind. I would not have wanted any more wine anyway. My head hurt from drinking it before and the pain from falling had made me dizzy and sick. I was so dizzy and sick that I thought I saw things once or twice in the edges of the lantern light. I had turned the lantern low so as not to wake John, and once I thought I saw an angel flapping down to snatch Mr. Watt off the deck but then I saw it was just the flapping edge of the sharkskin canopy.

The spilt malt fouled the fresh water, said Mr. Watt, *and that brought on a fever.*

Like whiskey flu! said Lonny. Lonny held the wine jug out to me and put a finger to his lips. I shook my head no.

Up in the elbow crook was the rogue wave they were boarded by, said Mr. Watt.

Rogue wave! weakly echoed from the mast.

Is Ira lashed to the mast again? asked Mr. Watt, and Lonny said no rogue wave had ever boarded the ship in all his years. Lonny said John just had a bad case of whiskey is all.

Mr. Watt said rogue waves steal up on you, worse in the day than in the night, for some reason, Mr. Watt guessing that at night you are always sensing something out there, coming for you, but in day, in the broad light of day, bright sunny day with no storm not even a distant thunderhead setting down a gray squall like a pachyderm paw, a bright bright sunny day with the earth as ocean, you hear a distant approaching crackle, a thin sound, the only warning of an errant mountain of water moving from continental coast to continental coast, a mountain of water that could have started as a small wave from an iceberg calving at the pole, the dense, still blueness of the arctic water corrupted by an overburdening, a breaking in a glacial mass, and the wave begins, stretches, pulled into its stride by the moon, warmed by the sun, saddled with a cousin monsoon swell, also errant, the two sweeping over atolls that had tamed lesser waves into broken surf and foam, the two waves together building into one wave they say can travel the length of the earth and always its width, said Mr. Watt.

Rogue waves always the worst in the broadest light of day when you hear them crackle behind you just as you reach for a crimping tool to fasten the end of a cotton sack full of shellcut and fillet, the sun on your naked back hot and your face cooled by the frosty smoke of ice in the open hold where your partner is handing down the other last cotton sack you have already crimped closed; a crisp, crackling sound you think for a moment is just a day at the beach, just the sound of surf beginning to tumble and break, that crackling sound, until you realize you are hundreds of miles from a shore and the horizon is heaping up on you, a sky of beautiful transparent green, and you look up and see a bright shimmering rainbow arcing in the crest of breaking spray taller than twice your mast, and you think *I will soon lose this crimping tool overboard*, and you think *My most merciful God, the hatches are open*, and you think *Soon I must embrace the ship*, and you think *It is not coming for me, it is coming for everyone*, the way the wave came for John and the ship he sailed on with bad whiskey fouling the drinking water, a rogue wave, John said, that he saw throw its leg over the rail like a thief stealing aboard before it collapsed on him and on his shipmates, splintering the decks and crushing the ship, rolling over, John saying his last image he could remember before he was blinded by the brine, the last image he saw so perfectly clearly, was the ship's hull so split in two like an oyster pried apart, the silvery pearl inside was the propeller still spinning three decks down just before the wave swallowed them and everything into a watery darkness.

Assa bunch of crap, said Lonny. *John got drunked up and fell overboard, everybody know that.*

Watch your mouth, Lonny, said Mr. Watt.

Rogue wave, said Ira Dench from the mast.

Yeah, rogue wave! said Lonny laughing. *Yeah, once*

I had a rogue wave come up out of the toilet. I was taking a dump the size of a palomino pony and a big rogue wave came up and splashed all over my balls! Come here and have a sit with me, Fishboy, Lonny said, and I stood a little closer to John with the lantern.

On the top of his arm, Mr. Watt said, you could see where John was foam-borne ashore a basaltic island, a red and black rock formation masoned with a pedestal and a chimney, the whole thing a small hillock in the ocean, the rogue wave depositing him there and continuing on for several days, and it was documented: seventeen ships and three thousand people lost in its wake, and it was documented: the rogue wave struck a direct hit into a trading town, the wave's foot surging along Nasty Place, a gamble-and-whore shantytown built on stilts and pilings, the rogue wave surge sucking at the rotten shore and pulling on the pilings until all the place folded over like a collapsing row of houses of cards, houses crowded with shouting and whoring embraces, bottles tilted, spilling, and men holding winning hands of cards over their heads as they were pitched into the torrent, and it was documented: the rogue wave sped up Main Street punching out plate glass windows and looting stores, the rogue wave climbing staircases and upending bedsteads, throwing respectable citizens in their pajamas and nightgowns out balcony windows and then leaping after them; the rogue wave turning left at the plaza, body-blocking and roll-tripping a string of horses tied in front of the jail, drowning inside the jail the entire El Fangado Gang in town to spring their retarded cousin Estebell caught shoplifting a bracelet, and it was documented: the mayor strangled at his breakfast table by an octopus, a shark seen eating grapefruit from a tree, sand dollars in the bank vault, and documented: the rogue wave, worn out by its global romp, staggers up Cathedral Street and falls in diminished supplication at the feet of a little girl sitting on the church steps sucking a carrot and holding a kitten, the rogue wave finally spent, licking briny kisses on the orphan's toes.

I just can't, I don't believe, said Lonny.

And Mr. Watt said the congregation, hearing the roaring through their town, threw open the church's doors and saw the ruin, the sea-swept town, the masts of ships tangled in the telephone wires, the little girl on the steps who had held back the waters and spared those of them in the house of their god, making the little girl a saint on the spot for it.

I just won't believe any of it, said Lonny, and Mr. Watt told him *Then just don't believe it.*

That girl became the biggest whore after that, said Lonny.

Mr. Watt went on. *In John's skin is the mark of the*

basaltic altar where John was thrown up by the rogue wave.

It was a volcano, said Lonny, his voice deep in the wine jug he was holding to his mouth. *Drunk overboard and pitched up on a volcanic island.*

John woke up, said Mr. Watt, *his head caught in a rock crevice, too weak to free himself.*

I know how a hangover like that feels, said Lonny. Lonny said for me to come sit beside him.

John on the downside of the altar rocks sometimes thinking he could hear a woman's voice, or it could be him delirious and just the wind moving through the crevice that held his head.

Or the rocks in his head, said Lonny.

And Mr. Watt said one day a face appeared peering down at him, a woman's face, all that he could see of her, and he called out but she disappeared. Later she came back and fed him raw strips of fish with her mouth in a funny kissing blowing way, and she poured fresh rainwater from a conch shell, poured it into his mouth and bathed his face for him and dried him with her hair. John said she was beautiful. John said she spent hours staring down at him and John made motions and spoke to her to help him pull himself out, and she did not seem to understand, and she never spoke to John and John could not touch her, and saw only her face as it appeared

185

every day between all the igneous rock. Had she a boat? he wondered, and that would be wonderful, he thought, to escape, the two of them in a boat, but she did not seem to appear from a boat, he never heard her approach until she was leaning over him, feeding him from her mouth to his mouth strips of raw fish, pouring rainwater from a conch shell, bathing his face, drying his eyes with her hair, staring at him for hours. And not a word, never a word, leaning into the crevice where he lay, feeding him, gently puffing on his lips, puffing and spreading his lips with her breath, until it was a kiss, a blowing kiss, and John's lungs filled with her breath, his lungs about to burst, his head lightening, his lungs growing daily so that by the time of a spawning moon, she smiled. The spawning moon pulled the tide around them like a bedsheet, and she lay with him, with the part of him that was free from the rocks, and John was frightened because the moon had pulled the water around them so that the sea spilled over his face and lapped along the edges of the rock. She lay with him and he was frightened that he would drown when the waves broke over his head, but he did not drown, his lungs were large with the way he had learned to draw air, large from her blowing kisses, and in this way, John began to learn rapture.

What a crock! said Lonny. *He got drunk, bumped*

his head, fell overboard, and had to dry out on an island. That's no real story, said Lonny. Come here, Fishboy, and let Uncle Lonny tell you a real story. Old Uncle Lonny here is the thirteenth son of a thirteenth son. I'm the rootin-tootinest, most ass-kicking, bull-whipping, hell-dwelling, cat-skinning, dog-kicking, grandma-down-the-stairs-pushing fellow you'd ever want to meet, so come be nice and give your old Uncle Lonny a little kiss.

Mr. Watt said that in the morning after the spawning moon John felt revitalized. His head and hair were slick from the waves soaking them all night. It hurt, but he was able to squeeze his head free of the place where it had been crush-cradled in the rock. John lay back down and waited to surprise the woman who had saved him. He waited until he saw her shadow on the rock wall and he sat up to kiss her, and sitting up to kiss her, he saw that she was not a woman.

She saw him see her and she fled, flipping and crawling back into the water at the rock's edge. She stopped and looked back once and John saw her pain, her pain at how he had first looked seeing her, her not all woman, not all fish.

You don't believe that story, do you Fishboy? Lonny said to me and Lonny tried to pull me to him.

Don't, I said.

All John will say, said Mr. Watt, *is that she was hairy where she needed to be hairy and scaly where she needed to be scaly.*

Mr. Watt said the top of John's shoulder would show the course of the white-hulled ship that rescued him, John out of his mind, calling his lover to come back, watching her circle the chimney rock but not coming out of the water, her face not angry or sad but set, and John felt like she was beckoning him to follow her, and he remembered stories of sailors being lured by sirens to their drowning deaths, and on the second day there were sharks around, always sharks around, and she seemed to barely keep ahead of the sharks, and for three days she circled the island and beckoned to John, and twice John started down to the sea, and twice John lost his footing and twice John lost his faith, the currents strong and the sharks large, and John would fall back and climb the chimney rock to wave his shirt for her to come back, and that is how a passing white ship saw him, waving his shirt, and they sent a launch ashore, shooting rifles into the sea around them, John screaming *No, no,* and they shot in the water where John's lover had been swimming because they said the currents were dangerous and the sharks were large, and when they reached John he fought them, and they beat him and put him in a straitjacket in the brig thinking he had drunk seawater and had gone insane.

I'm the nail-bangingest, bush-wacking, horse-stealing, baby-buggering, wife-beatingest whoremongerer you'll ever meet, Fishboy, Lonny said.

In the brig John wanted pen and paper, said Mr. Watt, but they wouldn't give it to him, so he begged a needle from the ship's Medicine Man and a tin of shoe polish from the boy who brought him his meals, and John made a record in his skin of where he had been, where he might find again the chimney rock island, every morning and evening asking the cabin boy their heading, where the sun was that moment, foreward, aft, off the port quarter, and in that way he made crude charts in his skin from his thumb and finger departure to his collarbone rescue.

The wine was on Lonny like it gets on some men, and Lonny began to rack himself with a mean sob. *Really,* said Lonny, *I'm just an eye-gouging, back-stabbing, low-down, mud-laying, pud-pulling cockbiter.*

Go easy on yourself, said Mr. Watt to Lonny. Mr. Watt said the design over John's left breast was the rough plotting of where the white-hulled ship was the day they aired John on deck and he jumped ship, he just leapt the rail and swam down under as hard as he could swim. He said the men aboard the white ship were angry and a couple of rifle shots spun plume in the water past him, but he swam deeper and deeper into the dark depths, realizing his lungs had no lack of breath, realizing this was what his lover had done for him with her kisses, he could have followed her had he not lacked the faith, and John swam down and sat on the bottom of the sea for a long time with his head in his hands, the white ship gone, sharks circling in the dark.

I'm just a simple-minded, turd-licking, sun-dried piece of shit, said Lonny. *No goddamn good at all, I tell you, I'm a story of no goddamn good at all, fucking jerk-off me me me!* he said. Lonny sobbed harder and tore at his shirt. He flung his empty gallon bottle of engine room wine against the rail so that it shattered, and the noise brought John wide-eyed awake.

O dear heavenly father, I confess, said John looking into the bright coronal bottom of the lantern I held over his head.

John, said Mr. Watt.

Poor Watt, dead too, said John.

John, said Mr. Watt.

Have mercy on his hideous hide, said John.

John, you're not dead, said Mr. Watt.

I'm not dead? said John.

You must have been dreaming, said Mr. Watt.

I was, said John. *It was the same dream.*

We were just checking the charts, said Mr. Watt.

I feel like we're on a good course, I feel hopeful, don't you, Watt? John said.

Yes, I saw all sorts of places to look, said Mr. Watt.

That's good, I'm hopeful, said John.

Me, too, said Mr. Watt. *I'm going back to the wheelhouse.*

Goodnight, said John.

Goodnight, said Mr. Watt, and I felt Mr. Watt's moist finger rake through my hair and turn my head forward to lead him back to the wheelhouse. Once he stumbled on the way and caught himself on my shoulder.

Blind as a bat, said Mr. Watt.

That's a rich one, Mr. Watt, I said.

*O*ur days drifted away like smoke. There was ample sun in a hot tin sky and no wind. John's net, impossible to haul in, thick with seaweed and barnacle crust, was an underwater sail that pulled us along as it was billowed by capricious currents. The ocean here was viscous and black, blended gray behind us by our propeller. John said we were in the horse latitudes, figuring our position by pinching a roll of his tattooed skin.

Horse latitudes, said the cook, and the cook wrote that down in his book of poetry in the galley. Every day the cook wrote a poem to his Negress wife and set it adrift in an empty bottle. Stuck as we were in the ocean, the cook's poetry bobbed around the ship. Often in the afternoons Lonny would plunk at the bottles with idle rifle shots from the crow's nest, shattering them to the bottom.

Lonny's rift with the cook began to widen the day after our first supper, when the cook served us seven-times-seven soup made from the sour leftovers, the starter stock being a wad of snot and a rotten toe. The things he added included the ruined shark steaks, a package of freeze-dried custard, a quart of vinegar, the last of my garden gourds, a barrel of gruel, and a turnip he found in a bedpan. I stirred the pot and scraped the muck off the bottom so it would not burn. The cook wrote his poetry. I saw that I was learning how to cook.

Horse latitudes, said the cook again, and he tinked his cheap pen against his chin.

At noon we hit an honest slick of horses. A herd of gnarled-hooved and spotted ponies floated around us, their bloated bellies torn open by sea vultures, eels spinning in their entrails. John said a becalmed horse ship would run out of hay and fresh water and throw the ponies over. The sea vultures scrawed around us and John made me stay in the galley so I would not be carried off. We shut all the portholes and stuffed gas-soaked rags around the vents against the stench.

The cook wrote down to his wife *There is no bird what not calls your name to me, There is no breeze that you are not fresh upon.* We gagged and listened to the featherings and flappings of the giant vultures on our deck, the vultures splattering the deck with equine droppings and regurgitated horseflesh.

Lonny had been right about the two men shackled together in the prison aquarium not making it through the night. The next morning one was floating in the lifeboat Lonny had filled with seawater, the man still shackled to his ruby-eating partner who sat shatter-eyed on the bottom, his skin turning to soft moon, his lips clung with bubbles. John drew one of Lonny's axes and severed the dead man's arm, then pulled it through the shackle. For a moment I thought of putting the dead arm in the cook's locker as a joke but that thought passed. We wrapped the dead one-armed convict in a canvas shroud and put one of Mr. Watt's ballast stones at his feet. Just before we were going to say a little prayer over him and drop him over the side, his moon-skinned partner climbed out of the lifeboat. His skin was so thin in places that he looked like a cousin of Mr. Watt's. His most amazing aspect was not the purple and blue of his organs but the red ruby still stuck in his gut, a gem so fine that it seemed to pulse when the sun struck its facets, and it made it seem that the man's heart had fallen from his chest and beat in his bowels.

His skin dissolving, empty shackle dangling from his wrist, the ruby eater gathered up his shrouded partner and stood on the rail. He started to turn around to face us, as if he were going to make some pronouncement before he leapt, but the long-tormented Idiot strode forward and kicked them both over the side.

Horse latitudes, and the cook tinked his pen against his chin.

In the horse latitudes I stood on the oven stirring the soup with the boat paddle spoon, my legs braced against the screen door springs that the cook had secured the pot handles to the stove's top with. I stood trying not to splatter anything on my sharkskin shirt and my sharkskin pants and my sharkskin jacket that John had cut for me from the skin of the carcass that still flapped as a canopy over our deck. Already I had ruined the knees of the pants scrubbing the galley floor, and my sharkskin cap with the sharktooth decoration on the front had fallen into the soup and was another secret ingredient in the seven-times-seven soup. It was the adding of these secret ingredients that I was certain was condemning me to learn to cook. It was also leading to the widening rift between Lonny and the cook. The cook had told me to get some flour, so I took down the sifter and also the wooden mallet used to pound out the flesh of salted meat. I opened the dry locker, and there was the rat in the flour. *SO!* he said, and before he could tell me not to fuck with him I flattened his rat head with the mallet so hard that his legs pointed in all true directions, true north, south, east, and west. I picked up Mr. Rat by the tail and Mr. Rat became a seven-times-seven secret soup ingredient too.

That afternoon I stood on the stove and stirred the soup, stirred the soup, scraping the muck off the bottom so it would not burn. I turned the stove burner down; the galley was stifling with us all in there waiting for the horse stench to pass, waiting for the sea vultures to leave.

In the corner, Lonny had started teaching the Idiot his knots. Lonny had been leaving me alone, and I was glad for it but a little jealous of the Idiot too. Lonny had started remarking what a fine gentleman the Idiot was, and Lonny began to teach him his knots. The very first knot had been stumping the Idiot for days. Lonny said an easy way to remember how to tie a bowline was to make a loop and with the free end say *The rabbit comes out of*

*the hole, goes around the tree, and then goes back into
the hole.* Every time he handed the piece of rope to the
Idiot and said *Remember the rabbit,* the Idiot would hold
the soft rope to his neck and sob. *What an idiot,* said
Lonny finally.

John was spending time in the wheelhouse with the
blind Mr. Watt. They would listen to what they called
the comedy channel on the radio together and I could
hear them laughing. The cook sat at the galley table,
making silent words with his lips as he wrote in his book.
*Pony waves breaking, In a neigh of frolic, Tails of spray,
Manes of foam, Horse latitudes,* he said, tinking, tinking.

I helped the cook ladle up the seven-times-seven
soup for dinner. We all ate at the galley table, me, John,
Lonny, the Idiot, and up from the depths, still smoking
and complaining about the net's drag on the engines,
Black Master Chief Harold. The cook always picked up
his rusty meat cleaver whenever the bolts on the engine
room hatch blew open.

The cook ate standing near the sink, and at about
his third spoonful he started hawking, and Lonny threw
himself back in his seat and said *Oh for the love of
fucking god,* and the cook hawked and hawked, but this
was not the hawk of his cigarette smoke or the hawk of
something hung in his chest, this was the hawk of something caught in his throat, and just as Lonny was about

to seize the cook, the cook spit something into the sink, and I am sure he only spit into the sink instead of the pot because other people were present. He dug around in his spit with his finger and held up a small bone hardly an inch long and looked at it. I knew a rat bone when I saw one and I think so did the cook. He turned and looked at me and I dug my spoon a little less deep in my bowl for another bite.

After supper John stood at the porthole. The sea vultures had left without our noticing it, and now in the darkening sky golden lightning pitchforked in the distance. *I told you the weather was about to break,* John said to Lonny. After the men left to hose the vulture leavings from the deck the cook and I cleared the galley table. As I poured the barely eaten bowls of soup back into the pot, the cook stood looking out the porthole. *A black horse sky,* he said.

I took a bowl of soup up to the wheelhouse for Mr. Watt. He was still listening to the comedy channel. *Come in, come in, Fishboy, I can tell it's you by the smell of that sharkskin suit.*

I stayed for a while and listened to the radio. It was mainly voices and static, voices overlapping, some that sounded afraid and some outright shouting in distress. There were SOS calls, some saying they had lost their mast, some saying they had lost their rudder, some saying they were going down altogether. There were pleas for help, pleas for mercy, pleas for mothers and sweethearts, for other ships and other men, and behind the voices I could hear wind ripping and thunder rumbling and the static of lightning striking the water.

Mr. Watt answered each call holding his goopy microphone, Mr. Watt saying *Hang on, help is on the way!* or *Have faith, we are your rescue!* or *We are the light and the way, have faith!* and at the end of every one of his transmissions the weary voices would answer back *Bless you's,* and *Thank God's!* and Mr. Watt laughed and said *Isn't it rich? Things could always be worse!*

I went aloft with a bowl of soup for Ira Dench. The sea vultures had torn out his eyes and still he said he saw a rogue wave coming. I climbed past him and sat in the foul crow's nest to watch the rest of the dark descend upon us. I was as lonely as a sparrow on a rooftop.

*T*he thing that swam into our net during the storm left us with no steerage, the thing's swimming strength having pulled our ship over, so that we were running on our side. We had been riding out an errant thunderhead in the galley when we all felt the net yank at the ship, then yank at us again until the pull became steady and in a slow way everything teetered and slipped off everything else it had been resting on. Knives on the pegboard dove at us like a carnival trick and the plate lockers swung open their bay doors and bombed us with crockery. It was worse for the cook because the soup slid off the stove and the broth splashed hot around our legs, but the dregs, the clumps of soup matter that had clung to the bottom beyond the reach of my boat paddle spoon, fell thickly and slid across the galley table which was up-ending as we held on to it, and we saw it all, the rat skeleton remains, the bootlaces, the small shark carti-lages from when John had hung a pregnant shark from a rope and had broken her open with one blow — a primor-dial piñata, the cook had said — the unborn thrown swim-ming in the bubbling broth, the toe joint on the fetish string, many things I could not tell what they were even though I had probably put them in. But what Lonny saw that set him off was the honeycombed spans of coagu-lated hawk he knew had come from the coughing cook, and even as the ship listed from the yanking of the net, Lonny made a grab at the cook's Big Miss Magine—con-toured form saying *The fucking bastard has been spitting into the soup all along!*

Lonny fired the cutting torch after chasing the cook out the rotating portal of the aft cabin door. We were knee-deep in seawater and sideways as the thing that had swam into our wide net swam harder to get away from us. Lonny fired the cutting torch to cut loose the cable between our ship and the net so that the cookbutchering field of the aft deck would be level. John doused the cutting torch twice, pinching it like a candle flame telling Lonny that they may have netted the largest shark they had ever netted before. Lonny dropped the cutting torch and took up one of his axes which slid past him as the ship rolled farther on its side. He had caught a glimpse of the cook's Big Miss Magine dress going into the tool-shed. *Spitting in the soup,* he said. He said it was unbearable.

Unsinkable is what Black Master Chief Harold said we were not when he came up from the engine room. He said the engine room had flooded and the boilers were out. Behind the master chief the fire lackey and the boiler devil were bringing up the chief's restored motorcycle suspended between them on a pole. The foot pegs were catching in the doorway. *Put it in the large lifeboat,* Black Master Chief Harold told them.

The cable running down to the net shuddered as the big thing swam higher in our net pulling us farther over. Our smokestacks were tipping and Ira Dench, lashed to the mast, was about to drown in the tops of some very small waves.

This is the biggest shark I have ever caught, said John.

Black Master Chief Harold said that was all well and good, but that belowdecks it was hopeless. *I'm getting the boys to put my bike in a boat and we'll be off,* said the master chief.

At that moment the sun freed itself from the pack of storm-cloud stragglers and its rays threw deep shadows around us. The master chief and his crew put the bike in the crazily leaning lifeboat, and Lonny began to chop down the door to the toolshed. John watched for the fish that was pulling us as it began to surface. Lonny stopped his chopping to watch as the big fish first surfaced a huge black shark snout, blowing foam, angry with air, heaving and churning the water white until the fish's length, which was about ten of our own, broke out onto the surface. Its dorsal fin had a number on it and fumes escaped its gills and vents.

I smell atomic smoke! said Black Master Chief Harold.

Our cable went slack as the big fish slowed, and slowly our ship began to right itself. Ira Dench swept skyward again out of the drowning wave, and the Idiot now head down in a deck plate that had just been a porthole. The fire lackey and the boiler devil were pinned under the lifeboat and the master chief scrambled astern to snatch John's spyglass.

Our net seems to have fouled their propeller, said the black master chief.

This is the largest shark I have ever caught, said John.

Good gracious! said the master chief. *It seems they've caught fire!* he said.

I could see it, men opening hatches on the back of the giant steel fish, men climbing out, luminous smoke rushing their backs.

John rang our haul-back siren. *Haul back! Haul back!* he said. *Black Master Chief Harold, prepare to haul in the net!* he said.

Black Master Chief Harold supposed that if we hand-pumped the bilges and found some dry wood for the old number-three boiler, he supposed he could get the winches to turn a little bit. *Besides,* he said, *I'd like to get a look at their ark engine.*

*B*y dark with the Idiot and myself on the hand pumps, the engine room was only waist-deep and the number-three boiler had fired. Lonny engaged the winches and John threaded aboard the cable with a pike, pulling along lengths of it bare-handed. Our ship did not haul in the net as much as we drew ourselves closer to the big fish. We could see it better now; in the dark the fish had turned on a great spotlight, an electric eye illuminating itself as men worked with cutting tools and torches to free the fish's tail from our large net. Forward on the fish men still climbed from the skin followed by a kind of smoke that glowed in the sky, and we watched, as we neared, men in white suits being laid in rows on the forward snout, and even from our distance I could see that they had dim blue halos, and I pointed this out to John and asked him if those men were angels.

John kept saying this was the largest fish he had ever caught in his entire life.

About an hour's cable length away there was a sharp concussive blast belowdecks and our number-three boiler coughed a ball of fire that rolled from our stack and lit our place in the sea. The electric eye of the great fish followed the route of our cable from where it was wrapped around its own rudder back to our winches. Bullets began to swarm around our heads like bees until the riflemen found their range, and then slugs sprayed and splattered around us.

A real fighting fish, John said. He sent Lonny to

gather his axes and the grappling gear. I was to fetch a mattress to rip stuffing from to plug bullet holes, and find some gunpowder for disinfectant, John saying that if he got shot up a lot not to put too much stuffing in the bullet holes of his flesh and not to put too much powder in either to cauterize, saying *Remember, Lonny, that fellow once they stuffed with a bad gut wound, and they packed him with stuffing and a horn of powder to sear shut the wound, and when the cabin boy lit him off it was better than Celebration Day, and people on shore thought it was some sort of fireworks display.* Lonny said that was funny all right, and Lonny began remembering the time they put dynamite in the firewood at that lady's house and John said they should hurry along, he still had his hair and nails to do.

I helped John do his hair, weaving thick wet fuses in his beard and head, and then I fetched a rasp, a planer, and a rattail file so John could put an edge on his fingernails. In the hour before sunrise he lit the fuses, for fierceness, he said, and practiced growling until he was hoarse.

The sun gathered itself to climb over the horizon and we were ready. We waited. As we were struck by the dawn we saw the big iron fish foundering dead in the water, its hatches sprung, that spooky smoke thinning from its scuppers and scales. We watched as the last of its crewmen dropped themselves into a black rubber raft to join a small flotilla of black rubber rafts that drifted off into the distance and over the horizon. John sounded our haul-back siren, and the noise roused the men in the last black rubber raft. They lifted their sick, blue-haloed heads and shook their dimly glowing fists at us. Either their weakness or their fear of puncture kept their pistols holstered and their throwing knives sheathed, and unsheathed here came the bladder dagger in the teeth of the naked cook as he climbed over the rail, just as Lonny had put down his axes to finish hauling back the net. The cook had left his Big Miss Magine dress in the toolshed to fool Lonny and had pulled himself hand over hand along the outside rail hull and had hidden in the sea grass that grew along the waterline of our ship like a skirt. Here came the cook naked and covered with red sores, his bladder dagger unsheathed and clenched in his teeth, and there stood Lonny, as there stood us all, being boarded by our own cook, Lonny unprepared and caught unawares as the unsheathed blade was pulled by the cook from the cook's mouth and thrown with a skill that wheeled the sharpened steel through the air with Lonny the only thing in the way of where it would go, and Lonny caught the sharpened steel like a man who has cut and killed with sharpened steel before, and Lonny caught the dagger from the air, snatching it out of space, and hardly had the dagger left the cook's hand when Lonny snatched the knife from the air and in a small imitation of his own ax-spinning windmill trick, Lonny spun the thing back at the cook who was still seeing the image of the knife going away when the knife returned to bury deep between the eyes that now no longer saw.

Turnabout's fair play, said John.

As we looked at his nakedness before stuffing him into the pot and fastening the lid with screen door springs we saw that the cook's body was covered with sores, not the kind that he had come aboard with, not the bee stings, not the wasp and hornet stings, but fresh broken-skin sores, red and runny, that after careful scrutiny John and Lonny both leapt back and said *Pox!* Lonny saying *And he spit in the soup! I should have killed him sooner! God gives us food and the Devil gives us cooks!* And clamping down the lid and stretching the fastenings closed, John dropped the pot depth-charge–like over the rail, forgetting to puncture or weight it, and it floated like a barrel. Lonny gave it a blast with the musket from the crow's nest which only blew the lid off so that once more we had to consider the cook's fat face, the tongue-puffed cheeks, the eyeballs rolled dagger-ward.

John and Lonny engaged the growling winches that

drew in the last of the net cable, our ship easing along the tail of the big iron fish. John fanned the lit fuses in his beard, effective to frighten knaves and the learned alike, he said. He cinched his muleskin, tossed the grappling hooks, and stepped aboard the big fish's spine.

There was no resistance as John and Lonny challenged the open hatches, Black Master Chief Harold directing Lonny to the hatches over where he thought the engine room of the big fish would be. When the way was shown clear, the master chief laid a ladder from our ship onto the skin of the iron fish and climbed across, a two-shot lady pistol in his belt and a crescent wrench stuck in his back pocket. He hauled across his lead-lined suitcase, drew a deep breath, and disappeared down a smoking hatch in the fish's tail.

John and Lonny walked forward, climbed the dorsal fin, and descended a ladder out of sight.

The wind freshened while we waited, me, the Idiot, the boiler devil, and the fire lackey. The wind tipped the large seven-times-seven soup pot in which the cook had been stuffed. We could hear sharks striking at the pot to get at the meal within, their strikes sounding like dull punches on a muted bell. Our ship and the big iron fish hung together by the grappling hooks and lines which tightened and slackened and tightened more as the wind freshened again. The afternoon went on, the sun beginning to beam beyond us, looking way over our shoulders into the distance. The Idiot hid in the small lifeboat, peeking over the side in his sheriff's-star cap, his nose resting on his hands. I made a nest from the mattress stuffing and dozed, waiting for John and Lonny to reappear; the only signs of their wandering within the huge fish were things they made happen outside it. As they wandered, they pulled levers and turned valves that made hatches open and close, stabilizers creak up and down, water bubble near the bow. Once I heard the grind and click of a dead electric engine.

I dozed, and I slept until I felt it become much cooler, and I woke up when the sun began to set and the wind began to blow steadily. Cursing came to us, first from Black Master Chief Harold fumbling with his weird luminous luggage up the aft hatch, busted knuckles, knots on his forehead, and no help from the fire lackey and the boiler devil asleep near me. Then there was cursing forward, and the last of the setting sun set on John wiggling through a hatch and bringing up the lifeless form of Lonny behind him.

Damn god and dogs and goddamn! said John,

Lonny adrip in his arms, them both slightly aglow as John brought the body aboard and laid it in the stern.

John could not believe it as he paced back and forth, ripping the butt ends of the fuses from his beard. *I can't believe it,* he said. He said he found the big fish was entirely abandoned forward, and abandoned all the way aft until he passed into a small chamber where a small bald man sat at a table drinking tea, a peculiar knife placed on a plate before him. When John asked the man who he was, the man replied in a language that John did not understand, but the man motioned for John to sit down and have a cup of tea and John did. Then Lonny came up from another direction and he and John asked the man more questions to which they could not understand the answers until it occurred to John that the man was the captain and that he and Lonny were intruding on a ceremony in which the captain would kill himself with the ritual knife and then go down with his fish. John said *Lonny, let's go and come back later when the man is through,* and Lonny said *Sure,* and just as they bid the man farewell and turned their backs on him the small man took up the knife and slipped it into Lonny's back, pushing it to the hilt so that the point of the blade came out near Lonny's collarbone.

I couldn't believe it! said John. He said that after he finished shredding the small bald man with his fingernails and feeding him his own heart, he broke open the cabinets in the small chamber looking for something to stanch Lonny's wound with, and he found crocks of food and pots and pans. They weren't in the captain's ritual chamber, they were in the galley and the little man was just the cook the crew members had left behind! *I couldn't believe it!* John said.

Mr. Watt had come groping along the rail in the settling darkness. His obvious tear ducts had begun to swell, him hearing Lonny was dead. Even so, he had to turn away when he heard how Lonny had met his end and cough down a snicker, and John looked at Lonny and looked away, a smile wiped from his face, too. *The King of Cookbutchery killed by a cook!* said John. *Poor Lonny,* we all said.

We laid Lonny out on the hatch. I helped John take down the sharkskin canopy that flew over our deck and John spread the skin with two long bin boards. We lashed Lonny to this cross and John bridled this kite with net cable. Lonny was ready to launch.

In a few tries the wind caught the flapping folds of Lonny's shark shroud and billowed them out. Lonny and the kite lifted from the deck as John let line roll off the cable drums. Lonny, a little luminous, soared back and forth over us as we said goodbye. The wind that lifted him also parted us from our drifting, sinking prize. *Goodbye, Lonny, old friend,* said John, his foot on the drum brake easing out more line. *God have mercy on your soul,* he said.

John took his foot completely off the drum brake and let all the cable out. Lonny eased higher and higher into the stars. His only hope for heaven, said John as he finally cut the cable.

O n the third day after we had captured the prize fish and lost Lonny, Mr. Watt told me that John's quaking cough reminded him of a crocodile's bark. He had heard plenty once, gone inshore on a mail-packet boat to find a doctor. He had caught a ride inshore after they had taken a prize ship that had the governor's pregnant daughter aboard, in labor. How she cursed her husband, *You son of a bitch, goddamn you, knocking me up* and so on, and the fellow, he was a gent really, would turn to take a step out of the cabin and the governor's daughter would sit up in the bunk and say *Don't you DARE leave this cabin, you goddamn so and so,* said Mr. Watt, Mr. Watt smiling to remember it, starting to laugh a little and then seized by a similar bout of coughing. We were all coughing, all of us except Black Master Chief Harold, the fire lackey, and the boiler devil, all dead, and John, getting worse. *That mail-packet boat overshooting the landing in the dark and running aground, the splash of crocodiles in the water around them, and the way the crocodiles barked, quite like John's cough now,* said Mr. Watt, *like a croaking rupture in something large and muscular, and there wasn't a doctor in the whole country, come to find out. That was a bad business with the governor's daughter. There's a whole mapped length of John's flank we'll never sail in again. Hung and heads piked is what we'll get,* said Mr. Watt.

Mr. Watt, as weak as he was, melting like red wax on the deck, was arranging me and the Idiot and a few spare provisions in the small lifeboat, the shakes and chills on us even under the hot glare of the afternoon sun. Shakes and coughs and chills, red blistering poxes, worse-looking on Mr. Watt's corrupted membranes. The Idiot seemed not to be afflicted, he had not gone down with us into the engine room to see about getting up some power from the new ark engine, down there finding Black Master Chief Harold huddled inside the number-three boiler trying to stave off the shakes, the fire lackey and the boiler devil laid dead about, their skin hot radiant red already, Black Master Chief Harold's chattering teeth saying he had actually been uncertain about unpacking his lead-lined luminous luggage in front of them, the fire lackey and the boiler devil having tried to cut down a small diesel cylinder casing, the master chief percolating crude heavy water through a teapot, trying to regulate the reactor pressures, he said, the chain reaction series in a line of paint cans, but when it came down to it, said Black Master Chief Harold, him in his engine room lit by the light of the open valise, when it came down to it, he said, even with his mail-order manuals and science magazine articles, he said he really had absolutely no idea of what he was doing, and the damn chilling shakes would not stop, so why didn't we just drop the whole notion overboard, why didn't we? There were fresh leaks around the propeller, the bilges were flooding, but the master chief said he would be fit and on deck in time for tea later, just as soon as he warmed up a bit. Please, could we just close the door to the furnace as he crawled inside it on our way out, thank you, and we did.

Mr. Watt, bare-headed, arranged some flasks of precious fresh water for the Idiot and me and some leftover rotting fish from the hold for us to nibble on. Mr. Watt buttoned up my sharkskin shirt to its top sharktooth buttonhole. He straightened my sharkskin jacket, creased out the lapels, patted my head with his sticky mucous hands, his own head bare and searing under the sun. With the outbreak of pox, his long fine silver hair had come out in clumps in his brush the night before when he was sitting on the hatch with the rasping John, Mr. Watt startled at first pulling out the strands, then even in the dark I could see the resolve settle over him never to let life see him like that, so that in my satchel under my seat in the lifeboat he put his brush with the letter of his mother's name on the handle, Mr. Watt letting the evening breeze scatter his silver hair in glittering strands over the water.

Mr. Watt told me he was sorry the ship had never had a proper doctor aboard, but that really, in civilized countries, when they have the pox, they don't send doctors to afflicted villages, they send soldiers, and the soldiers surround the village and shoot anyone who tries to leave, and after a few days, when everyone is dead, the soldiers burn the villages, *That's the way it's done in civilized countries,* said Mr. Watt, and Mr. Watt said he thought that was how we had come across the cook, the cook fleeing a pox village with his buckboard, his Negress princess, and their family of griffe children when the rain and landslide caught them and swept the cook to sea, Mr. Watt's speculation interrupted by another of John's coughing fits, this one getting John up on his feet, coughing, coughing, trying to clear lungs that could hold days and weeks of air.

Look away, Fishboy, said the blind Mr. Watt, so I watched where small fish were resting in the shade of the silver raft of Mr. Watt's hair floating on the ocean.

In a while we heard the sound of water splashing the deck, and I thought it was because we were sinking, the ocean coming in through the scuppers. When I turned to look, I saw that the sound was coming from John again, John had coughed and coughed and ruptured his lungs, with each breath his heart pumped blood through his nose and mouth, and John would not let Mr. Watt near him to comfort him, John weak and leaning by the rail, the deck awash and slick with his blood, the blood frisky and running in rivulets, pouring out the stern and staining the sea, each breath more blood, and John watched and waited, waited for it to stop, and it did not stop, his beard and chest and the whole world charted on his body flooded with blood, and in the waters around our ship sharks began to cruise, around the stern where the water was reddest, they filtered the blood through their gills and snapped their tails in excitement, the bold ones snuffling the hull and the young ones leaping and plunging, rolling over the bloodstain on their backs like dogs on a spot of scent in grass, and John watched them, and sometimes when his throat filled with black hawk, he summoned it up and spit it in their eye. The hour grew late and I watched and the sharks waited, and still John breathed and bled.

Don't shame him by staring, Fishboy, Mr. Watt said to me, *You always were one to stare with that loose rolling eye.* Mr. Watt began to settle the Idiot into his place in the small lifeboat, the Idiot still managing to step on my broken feet, the Idiot was frightened, holding a blanket poncho and a length of string he kept shoving at Mr. Watt, and I think in Idiot-talk he was saying *Rabbit, rabbit,* looking for reassurance in a piece of looped string. Mr. Watt collected the Idiot's toys, the crushed fetish figures and my little broken coconut boat with the red swizzle-stick mast that I saw Mr. Watt had forgotten was my toy first.

In two ways I saw that Mr. Watt thought that we would never make landfall, would never have rescue. First it was with the oars, Mr. Watt trying to show the Idiot how to fit them in the oarlocks, how to sit in the cross seat, how to dip and pull the grips, but the Idiot pressed the string to Mr. Watt saying *Rabbit, rabbit,* his excited two-note whistle blowing slick through his bubbling lips, and Mr. Watt stored the oars in the bottom of the lifeboat, shaking his head.

And then second, as he settled the Idiot, I saw Mr. Watt's hands touch the sheriff's star pinned to the peak of the Idiot's cap, and Mr. Watt took the cap off to remove the incriminating evidence, and the Idiot shrieked and brayed so loudly like a donkey that Mr. Watt said *All right, all right,* saying it in a way that meant it really wouldn't matter after all. The Idiot, instantly comforted by his cap back on his head, pushed the string into Mr. Watt's drippy fingers, saying *Rabbit, rabbit,* and Mr. Watt carefully bent a right-turned loop and with the free end said *The rabbit comes out of the hole, goes around the tree, and back into the hole,* a bowline, and the Idiot clapped as Mr. Watt's eyes rolled upward, Mr. Watt fainting alongside our lifeboat.

I lifted my head to look at Mr. Watt, and at that moment a shudder struck the water and the sharks I could see turned and shot out in different directions. John, weak, also watched on the stern, staining everything with his blood as he breathed. In the sea of red, rumps of gray came humping toward us, scattering the sharks, bottle-nosed streaks of grace, the dolphins sending the sharks to flee to deeper depths, threatening with their shark-ramming snouts. A way was parted off our stern as if we had a wake, as if our propeller were not frozen in broken engine wreckage. John staggered and bled. He watched and I watched, and in our wake swam a woman, and the woman swam right for us until she was in the water beneath our rail and only John could see her, looking down. He looked down and wept with joy, trying to make words to thank God skyward, but his throat was choked by the racking bloody cough, and he barely had the strength to shed his muleskin cloak and climb the rail, but he did, and he let himself fall into the sea off our stern. I could hear him trying to exclaim and trying to breathe, knowing he still bled, and in their embrace they drifted away a little, and I could see them, I could see the woman and she seemed old, her hair was very gray, and she saw me looking and she smiled at me, and I saw her teeth were like dog's teeth. She made a way to hold on to John, her arm around his neck in a rescue of embrace, John lying on his naked back in the water breathing blood. I saw as she began to swim away with him that she was not entirely woman, and all I can say is that she was woman where she needed to be woman and something else where she needed to be something else.

And she started to swim away with John under her arm, leaping dolphins leading, and in the last of John's face I could see deep rapture, his broken lungs and heart still pumping a trail of red that followed them toward the setting sun, John's dimming eyes seeing mine, and his arm, the one on which his story began, rose and fell with every wave and powerful stroke his woman put them through, and the way his storied arm rose and fell I did not know if he was beckoning me to follow or just waving goodbye, and weak, I just watched as they bled away from us, the sea deep crimson, the bloody foam coughed from his lungs rising in cumulus tiers towering in the sky, the pink froth brilliant, the warm red stains finally extinguished with the setting sun.

The sea began to flood our sinking decks. Mr. Watt awoke in the briny chill and stumbled groping for John in the stern. He picked up John's muleskin wrap, and felt it, saying *Poor John, gone to fight one last fish,* and I was too weak myself to tell him what I had seen. Mr. Watt put the muleskin around his shoulders, thought differently, and then came and laid it over me in the bottom of the small lifeboat. Mr. Watt pushed the boom over, broke the davits, and cranked our craft into the ocean. *I would have put you in the big lifeboat,* he said, *but Black Master Chief Harold's damned hobby project is in it and I'm too tired to move a motorcycle tonight. I'll lower it with Ira Dench in it, and maybe somebody will spot the two boats instead of just the one.*

Mr. Watt kissed my head before he shoved us off, saying *May your bowstem break in bulrushes.*

In the dark ocean I could hear the Idiot turning around in his seat in fear, making odd noises, standing up enough to rock the boat, banging me from side to side in the bottom, stepping on my feet and legs. The Idiot quieted briefly when we heard Mr. Watt's faint voice across the water. We heard Mr. Watt say *Come on now, Ira, stop this nonsense, I'm going to put you in the damned boat, don't fight me,* and it must have been just when Mr. Watt untied Ira Dench from the mast that the rogue wave struck us, I heard its curl and the stars were blanked, and the falling phosphorescent foam lit the Idiot's bug-eyed upturned face one instant before the wave rushed down upon us, sending us surfing across the sea.

The rogue wave that carried us was more a carousing straggler, more a careless wanderer borne off the storm front from a few days before, more of a shouldering encouragement than a wall of charging foam. We traveled in its gurgling crest for two days before it lay suddenly spent on the ocean, mingling itself on an upper current, laying itself to rest.

By then the Idiot had either drunk or spilled the flasks of fresh water Mr. Watt had filled for us without offering me any as I lay sick in the bottom of the lifeboat. When it was cool in the evening he took my muleskin. Unable to tie it around his waist, he draped it forgotten on a gunwale and it was soon overboard. He once or twice nibbled at the souring fish we carried and then played with them in the water, leaning over so that his big butt mooned hairy and pimpled. He leaned over, almost capsizing us, playing with the dead fish in the water, flapping the flatfish around until something large and toothy made a rush from below and the Idiot came away with bloody nipped fingertips. That was the end of playtime.

The chills and fevers were still on me; my body was corrupt. My fingers were not strong enough to unbutton my sharkskin clothes. In the afternoon of the third day my sleeps became deeper and I felt my life closing. I fell asleep once and was awakened by feathers brushing my face. When I opened my eyes I saw a man in white robes rowing our boat, the wings that sprouted from his back wagged against my face as he bent to dip and pull the oar handles. I tried to call out. The man turned and looked at me and I saw that the man in white robes had the Idiot's face and blubbering mouth, the distended tongue that now, when I listened, whistled the two-note work of rowing. I fell back asleep. I felt the feathers again. I opened my eyes and a seagull was sitting on my chest pecking at the sharkteeth buttons of my sharkskin suit.

The Idiot's eyes were focused far ahead and I hoped, by the Idiot's look and by seeing the bird, that land was near. The Idiot sat and grunted, sitting in the stern seat, his hands on the rails and rocking us so that the afternoon sky waved back and forth. The Idiot sat holding the lifeboat rails like he had held on to the sides of the buckboard wagon John had brought him to the fishhouse lot in, and I wondered if he was going to spill us. Once, I felt our keel scrape, and I thought *Shallows!* and when the Idiot did not jump out, I thought *Sandbar,* and then I heard a familiar sound that I had heard in my outermost travels from my cartonated encampment, I heard sand waves and sea dunes folding over, and I smelled rotted marsh grass even over the stench of the souring fish and ourselves, and the seagulls began to hover and then hop around us, only the Idiot trying to catch one keeping them away.

The lifeboat leveled out now, out of the sea, and something went by chuttering, its wake rocking us, the Idiot following it with his eyes. Someone called out and offered us a tow, and the chuttering sound came around again, a line fastened on our bow. Soon I smelled fish guts and fresh fillet. I began to hear clattering sounds like plates and platters, I could hear scraping sounds like the workings of butter-turned knives. And then I heard my name. *Fishboy! More fish, more shellcut. Fishboy!* I tried to sit up and I could not, my body weak and my eyes dimming, only my orbiting eye having a turn of focus, focusing on the Idiot's face, the only mirror of our surroundings for me, and so I watched his face, and I watched it when it was startled as it was struck by a line thrown from the dock, and he picked it up and held it, and I felt us being drawn until our lifeboat was in the shadow of the pack-out pier of the fishhouse. And there standing over us was the red-rimmed drunkard, blind from the snake stick. He told the Idiot he was lucky, that this was the last boat they were going to pack out that day, and then I heard the red-rimmed drunkard say *Fishboy, drop a basket in here,* and another head appeared looking down, and it was the soft-skulled child, and then he was down in the bottom of the lifeboat with me, raking and shoveling the souring fish into the wire basket, and then struggling to put me into it too. The red-rimmed drunkard, hearing the child struggle, asked what kind of fish did he suppose I was, and the soft-skulled child said he supposed I was a red speckled something left out too long in the sun.

I was hauled up on the fishhouse pack-out pier by the rope boom and set down in the shade of a brand-new metal cutting shed, new raw wooden tables and chain-sawed beams, the wreckage of the old place burned by the weeping man who said *Fuck* and our ship's crew pushed into a charred pile in the corner of the fishhouse parking lot. I took my first look again at the big black women tabulating their work and collecting their chits from the red-rimmed drunkard, the Idiot standing stupidly by, the red-rimmed drunkard giving him two copper coins that the Idiot just stared at, *And not a cent more!* said the red-rimmed drunkard, the soft-skulled child shaking out the basket I lay in on the new concrete floor, him singing *Finish fish! Finish fish! Come and get your finish fish!* My fish-eyed look and sharkskinned appearance put the women off, as something inedible, them reaching around me for some of the other slimy fish, woman after woman spitting complaint at the poor pickings until I lay by myself on the concrete. Then bending over me was Big Miss Magine's ugly sister. She reached down and lifted me up, rolling me in her plastic-fronted apron, her finish fish of the day.

Big Miss Magine's ugly sister carried me as a bundle through the fishhouse lot, past where the soft-skulled child was building his cooking fire in his blackened board encampment with charred timbers salvaged from the fishhouse fire. There were his things, a broken deck chair, a bare-ribbed parasol planted in the sand to dry his one pair of socks and one brown shirt and his plastic-fronted apron. No garden yet, but I could see a seeded plot marked and guarded from rabbits with cast-off netting and pounded stakes.

I rode in the purple bus on our way around the cratered lake, laid in Big Miss Magine's ugly sister's ample lap, cushioned soft from the shocks to the springs and the tipping corners, hearing the gobbletalk, the light leaving the sky, the sun slipping, I knew, a figure eight of flame into the cratered lake. I got off the bus as the bundle beneath Big Miss Magine's ugly sister's arm, was taken to the outdoor sideboard to be unrolled and cleaned, but the sharkskin resisted the fish scraper, and she was tired from her day at the fishhouse, so I was brought in whole and laid on the counter until she could get the stone-scoured pot lit and boiling, and there she was, herself laid on an old rotten cot like she was a poured sleeve of tar, Big Miss Magine naked and lean, shriveled from her punctured guts, a yellow stained plaster applied to the hole my butter-turned knife had made. *This'll make a good soup cure,* said the ugly sister, patting me, talking in the way people talking to the dying talk after every remedy has been tried and every remedy has failed, and Big Miss Magine smiled and nodded and looked right into my rolling orbiting fish eye. And I lay on the counter a long time, long into the evening waiting for the solid stone-scoured pot to boil, and no matter how long or how often I looked away, I always turned my fish eye back to Big Miss Magine as she lay in her rotten cot, her big red-blue-purple egg of an eye staring straight back into my own. We stared until the ugly sister said my skin was too tough to gut and Big Miss Magine nodded to put me in the pot whole, this special red speckled something fish, organs and all, and the ugly sister slipped me into the stone-scoured pot and I felt myself slipping away, I felt myself leaving, even as the sharkskin suit floated away and my ears filled with boiling water, the white broth over my eyes, I could still see, the sight of my fish eye hovering over the scene below, I filled the room as curling lisps of steam, I could still see, and I even saw myself leak out of Big Miss Magine's butter-turned punctured gut and seep beneath the yellow plaster when her ugly sister held a bowl of my broth up to her lips to drink.

I am sometimes in the dune lines, and in the afternoons I am deep within the woods. I know the place where a cap with a sheriff's pin floats atop a quicksand pool, the Idiot chased there by men with bullwhipped dogs, betrayed by the fishhouse women who said a large man they had seen before had come ashore dressed in muleskin.

At dusk I wander the side road so that by evening you can find me at the edge of the soft-skulled encampment. I am the watching face that flickers just beyond the firelight. I come to study the child as he sips his finish fish soup. I listen for the fear in his voice as he calls out to me, *Who's there?* I watch him reach for the shovel of fire that brightens me away.

I mist inside your house. I linger in your curtains. I wait until you are asleep so that I can speak to you in your dreams. I am as close to you as the veins in your neck when I say to you, in my whispering lisp, *I, too, began as a boy.*

about the author

Mark Richard was born in Louisiana and raised in Texas and Virginia. At age thirteen he became the youngest radio announcer in the country, with a music and news show on WYSR-AM in Franklin, Virginia. He attended Washington and Lee University. After his third year there he left to work on oceangoing trawlers and fishing boats from Georges Bank to Cuba. After three years on the water he returned to school and earned a degree in journalism. Since that time, Mark Richard has been employed as a radio announcer, aerial photographer, house painter, advertising copywriter, naval correspondent for a newspaper, magazine editor, bartender, private investigator, and teacher. His short stories have appeared in *Esquire, Harper's, The New Yorker, Shenandoah, Grand Street, Antaeus,* and *The Quarterly,* and have been anthologized in *Best American Short Stories, New Stories from the South,* and the *Pushcart Prize.* His first collection of short stories received the 1990 PEN/Ernest Hemingway Foundation Award for best first published book of fiction.

Mark Richard lives in New York City. This is his first novel.